HITLER'S
OCCULT WAR

HITLER'S
OCCULT WAR

Michael FitzGerald

ROBERT HALE · LONDON

© Michael FitzGerald 1990
First published in Great Britain 1990
as *Storm-Troopers of Satan*
This paperback edition 2009

ISBN 978-0-7090-8871-4

Robert Hale Limited
Clerkenwell House
Clerkenwell Green
London EC1R 0HT

www.halebooks.com

A catalogue record for this book is available from the British Library

2 4 6 8 10 9 7 5 3 1

Printed in Great Britain by the MPG Books Group, Bodmin and King's Lynn

Contents

A Few Words on the Occult

What is 'the occult'? And does it work? These questions lie at the very heart of this book.

People's attitudes towards the occult have tended to fall into one of three groups; there are those who argue that such things as occultism do not and cannot happen; those who argue that all the phenomena of occultism are genuine, and those who, like myself, take the view that some of it is true and some false.

Most people have at least some idea of what the occult is. Astrology, tarot cards, foretelling the future, telepathy – all these and perhaps more would be quickly thought of by most people if they were asked. But the kingdom of occultism is far wider than simply those aspects.

My own view is that all occult phenomena are the result of activity within the human mind. We use about ten per cent of the powers of the mind, and of the remainder we are only dimly aware, if at all. And the evidence for some types of occult powers is so strong that, in any other science but that known as 'parapsychology', it would have been accepted long ago. But resistance to its acceptance is crumbling beneath the sheer weight and volume of the evidence; quantum physicists these days sound more like occultists than the old-fashioned Newtonian scientists.

In this book I demonstrate how the Nazis set out, in a systematic way, to apply occultism and magic for the purpose of gaining control of the whole world. That was their ambition, and occult weapons were as freely used by them as tanks and aircraft and rockets. Some of their ideas were plain dotty, like the enormous amounts of money they wasted in trying to 'prove' that the earth was hollow, and that we lived on the inside of it.

When they turned their efforts to other fields, such as the power of the human mind to control people and even material objects, some of their aims were only too frighteningly successful. So alarmed did the more thoughtful occultists become by their success in harnessing black magic to the goals of the Nazi war machine that they began to use their own white magic to counter it. When war broke out at last, the British in particular made extensive use of occultism to forge a new weapon against the Nazis. So too did the Russians and the Americans. The Nazis had their own Occult Bureau, the Ahnenerbe, on which they spent more money than the Americans did upon the atomic bomb.

Some of the material in this book is so weird that at times even I find it hard to believe. However, I have been careful to state exactly when I consider something to be true and where I regard it as being false. Not being given to either blind credulity or dogmatic scepticism, I have been able to adopt a rational approach towards my subject.

That the occult can work is certain, since it is nothing more than making use of certain powers which lie within the human mind. But that it cannot work without some sort of grip upon reality is also certain. Hitler could no more raise his fallen soldiers from the dead than he could use the inside of the hollow earth as a radar detector – one of the many less than sensible things which he tried to do during the war.

The reader of this book will discover exactly how big a part occultism played in the everyday thinking of the Nazi leaders. The most notorious example of this was during the Russian campaign, when Hitler's complete failure to equip his troops for the Russian winter was directly due to the occult weather forecasts he had received from Hoerbigerian disciples in the Occult Bureau. But the whole of Nazi thinking from first to last was based upon occult principles.

It cannot be too often stressed that the whole Nazi movement was deeply rooted in magic and the occult. Again and again I have demonstrated this fact in my book. Hitler, Himmler, Goering, Rosenberg and even Goebbels were all well versed in magical and occult learning. What may surprise readers even more is that Churchill, Roosevelt and Stalin also believed in, and made use of, occultism and magic as weapons to counter the

Nazi threat. I go into some detail about the nature and extent of Allied involvement in occult activities, an area which I believe I am the first writer to have dealt with.

Preface

Under the Nazis, most of Europe was ruled by men who dreamed of a giant leap forward in human evolution. The Nazi leaders really believed that they could bring into being a master race of supermen, not simply through a programme of deliberate selective breeding, but through the systematic use of magical skills to dominate men, machines and the material world itself. In their vision of a new heaven on earth, 'inferior' races were to be swept away by the sacrifice of their blood, and on the foundation of their deaths, a new world would come into being, a world peopled by a master race of men who had passed beyond all that humanity had reached before. The cold, hard brightness of this vision took no account of the suffering and death of millions of supposedly inferior beings.

To help them achieve this end, the Nazis harnessed not only a war machine of frightening power and efficiency, but any and every aspect of magical and occult technology. It did not matter to them that Western science, as well as the Western liberal-humanist tradition, rejected their vision. The Nazi leaders 'knew' that they had the truth. Western science they regarded as shallow, superficial and irrelevant. In the tragic grandeur of their flawed but powerful vision, Western science was a mere incident in human history. Their world would dwarf it with the splendour of its achievements. Or so at least, they thought.

To men caught up in such a vision of life, the deaths of millions seemed unimportant. This aspect of their thinking, more than any other, helps to explain what Hannah Arendt so aptly called 'the banality of evil'. At Nuremberg, when the surviving Nazis were put on trial for their crimes against humanity, it was obvious to observers that there was no common language of thought and feeling between the prosecutors and the defendants on the stand. The men and women on trial were listening to other voices. To them, the magical domination of the world was all-important.

Magic, of course, can be used to serve good or evil ends. The Nazis turned its powers to the service of evil; but among their opponents were many highly gifted magicians and occultists. They knew that the powers they possessed could and should be used in the service of good; and they turned their energies to seeing that they were so used. Many of them paid for their courage with their lives; but the victory was theirs in the end. In spite of all the vast magical skills at their disposal, the Nazis had forgotten that the fundamental law of magic is balance. They had chosen to serve power and reject love. But without love, no world worth having can ever be brought into being.

1 Hitler's Youth

Hitler may have literally drunk in psychic powers with his earliest milk. He was born at 5.30 p.m. on 20 April 1889, at Braunau-am-Inn, a place noted for its mediums. This Austrian frontier town was the birthplace of Madame Stockhammes, who married Prince Joachim of Prussia. Two more famous mediums born there were the psychic brothers Willi and Rudi Schneider.[1] And the Munich spiritualist Baron Schrenk–Notzing went to Braunau to recruit his subjects, one of whom was actually a cousin of Hitler.[2]

As if simply being born in medium country was not enough, Hitler shared another thing in common with the Schneiders. The same woman who wet-nursed Willi Schneider also wet-nursed Adolf Hitler; we can only imagine what impact that may have had upon him. Did Hitler grow up hearing stories about strange and slightly scary powers – and decide to master them himself?[3]

There is no question about Hitler's astonishing personal magnetism. He could transform crowds into hysterical worshippers, and also had the ability to dominate even the strongest men at close quarters. Yet physically he was anything but impressive. He was too short, dressed shabbily, his hair was a mess, his toothbrush moustache looked positively comical, and his walk was a cross between a mince and a shamble. When Chaplin filmed his brilliant satire on Hitler, *The Great Dictator* he had to change almost nothing to play the Nazi leader. Hitler really did look like Charlie Chaplin.

Another amazing thing is that Hitler was not at all a good speaker. He waffled, stammered and hesitated while he was getting himself worked up. But once he did get going, it was as if he had shifted into another gear. Suddenly power seemed to flow out of him, waves of emotion spreading out over the audience, raising them to a hysterical frenzy. At such times his charisma was absolutely irresistible. But it was not only on crowds that he could work his magic. Even men like Goering. Dönitz and von Blomberg were completely unable to stand up to him in person. And even when Germany was falling to pieces around Hitler and his followers, they still clung to the belief that somehow he could find a way out, as he had done so often in the past.

How was it that a man like Hitler could become dictator of Germany and master of much of the world? He looked comical, was a poor speaker, largely self-educated, came from a poor family and had been orphaned at the age of eighteen. Throughout his life, Hitler had few friends. He was not a good mixer, and completely lacked all the social graces. Hitler did not even have the money to effect a smooth entrée to the upper echelons of power. And yet he succeeded in ruling Germany and most of Europe. How was this possible?

For clues to how it was that such an unprepossessing figure became a world leader, we must begin by looking at his youth.

At school, Hitler was a mediocre pupil, who failed to distinguish himself in any subject except history. This may have had something to do with the fact that Hitler's history teacher was a fanatical racialist. Until the age of eleven Hitler was a devout Roman Catholic. Then his father fell ill. Three years later he was dead, but not before considerable suffering. Then Hitler's mother contracted breast cancer and he had to nurse her through the final stages of her illness. By the time he was eighteen, both Hitler's parents were dead.

He experienced a sudden revulsion against the Christian values with which he had been brought up. From that point on, he never spoke or wrote of Christianity except in terms of utter contempt. Hitler's attitude towards religion was further hardened by his discovery at this time of the philosophers Schopenhauer and Nietzsche. Together with the music of Richard Wagner they were to become a decisive influence upon his life.

From Schopenhauer he took the philosopher's pessimism and

his belief that life is a blind purposeless struggle of will. Schopenhauer denied the existence of God and proposed a system of morality based not on rules, rather on feeling. From Nietzsche he took the philosopher's contempt for weakness, and particularly for the way in which Christianity elevated it into a virtue. He also took over his concept of 'the will to power', the vision of life as an eternal struggle in which only the strong and heroic survive, and above all the vision of a race of supermen, pure and brave and strong.

Anyone who has studied the works of Schopenhauer and Nietzsche will see at once that Hitler simply abstracted some of their ideas and discarded all the ones that did not fit with his preconceptions. Nietzsche, for instance, described the Jews as 'the strongest, toughest and cleverest race in Europe'. Hitler had nothing but contempt for them, of course. Similarly, the dominating aspect of Schopenhauer's philosophy is his sense of tragedy, based upon a deep compassion for human suffering. None of this side of Schopenhauer comes through in Hitler at all.

Hitler's only close friend during his late teens and early twenties was August Kubizek, whom he nicknamed 'Gustl'. He managed to persuade Kubizek's parents to let him study music at a Vienna school. Hitler himself had applied to go to an art school there. However, unfortunately for him and possibly the rest of the world, he was turned down. Hitler was a talented painter and if he had been able to achieve recognition in this field it is possible that he would never have turned to politics. However, he was rejected, though Kubizek was accepted for his music course. Hitler's reaction was to do what would now be called defrauding social security. Since he was in receipt of his father's pension, but only so long as he was a student, he simply pretended that he had been accepted. For four whole years he managed to keep up this pretence until, at last, his fraud was discovered. Luckily for him, at this very moment his Aunt Johanna died and left him the bulk of her money. He was also making a small living by selling his pictures, and it was during this period that he became acquainted with a number of figures in the occult-racist underground of Vienna.

Another preoccupation of Hitler at this time was avoiding military service with the Austrian army. He spent five years dodging the call-up and living under a variety of aliases. At one point he even left the country altogether and went to stay with his half-brother in Liverpool, where he picked up a fair command of English.[4] A year before the outbreak of the First World War, Hitler went to Munich, where he seems to have felt much happier than he was in Vienna. However, at the beginning of 1914 he was finally arrested for his evasion of military service and only escaped imprisonment by a combination of lies, personal charm and an ability to malinger which he kept throughout his life. The result of these various ploys was that he was rejected by the Austrian army as being unfit to serve. And yet – one still wonders. Did Hitler simply set out to display his histrionic talents in a more exaggerated form than usual? Or did the army see signs of mental illness in Hitler?

Whatever the reasons for his rejection, and in spite of their being no noticeable change in his health during 1914, he was still accepted into the German army on the outbreak of World War I. Hitler was extremely lucky during the war, both on the personal level, since he served on the Western Front for four years without being killed; but also on the political level, since he was able to make contacts in the army which later proved extremely useful to him. For example, Hitler became friendly with Max Ammann, the company sergeant-major who published *Mein Kampf* during Hitler's imprisonment and who was later to become the business manager of the Nazi Party.

Within six months of the start of the war Hitler had been awarded the Iron Cross, second class. In the easy comradeship of soldiers and the military discipline he found qualities which up to then he had conspicuously lacked.

Further decorations followed: the Military Merit Cross, a citation for bravery and the Service Medal. At this point he was wounded and temporarily sent back to Germany for hospital treatment. On his return to the Western Front he was promoted to lance-corporal and took part in the last series of German offensives during 1918. In August of that year, Hitler was to win the Iron Cross, first class, under tragi-comic circumstances. His regiment was being mistakenly attacked by German artillery and, under heavy fire, he carried a message to them that they were shooting at their own men. Two months later he was gassed and again hospitalized.

While still recovering in hospital he heard the news that Germany had surrendered, the Kaiser had abdicated and with him the other German royal kings and princes. To Hitler, who not long before had seen the Germans apparently winning the war on the Western Front, it came as a shattering blow. He hid his face in the pillow and cried. All the soldiers' sacrifices, he thought, had been in vain; the politicians had let Germany down and betrayed her. At that moment he decided to go into politics himself.

The end of the war and the abdication of the Kaiser plunged Germany into a state of chaos. Civil war was very near. The Social Democrats had a majority in the German parliament and assumed power; but both left- and right-wing extremists repudiated the federal government. In Bavaria, a coalition of left-wingers ranging from Social Democrats to Anarchists took power. Before long it was fighting for its life: First its leader, Kurt Eisner, was murdered by a Count Arco–Valley, who was both a monarchist and a Jew; then the new Socialist leader was repudiated by his own party. A new government took over, consisting of Anarchists, Communists, and assorted left-wingers. This new regime lasted only a week before the Communists took sole charge of the government.

Meanwhile the forces of counter-revolution were being organized by the Thule Society, about which we shall have more to say later. They were an occult-racial movement to which many leading Nazis belonged at one time or another. Their most prominent member came to be, of course, Hitler himself.[5] The Thulists recruited ex-soldiers from the trenches into a *Freikorps*, a Free Corps, with the specific intention of suppressing the Soviet Republic.

In Munich, the power-base of the Communist regime, a 'red terror' was unleashed. The Red Army were just as ruthless in maintaining itself in power as the Nazis proved to be later on. Atrocities were committed by both sides and eventually the *Freikorps*, together with regular army units, fought their way into Munich and bloodily suppressed the revolution.

One of the most curious aspects of this 'Soviet Bavaria' is that there now seems little doubt that Hitler joined the Red Army and helped to maintain the Communist regime in power. During the recapture of Munich by *Freikorps* and army units,

Hitler was actually arrested by federal troops for firing on them as they entered the city. Again, however, Hitler's extraordinary luck held. He was recognized by some officers from his old regiment and whatever excuses he offered for his conduct were accepted. In fact, out of this fiasco, which could so easily have shattered his career for ever, he was able to build the first tentative foundations for his subsequent rise to power.

Because he had been in Munich, actively involved in the revolution, Hitler was assigned to a military commission set up to investigate the events. Hitler took the opportunity to betray as many former comrades as he could recognize and was rewarded by being sent on an army training course in politics. This gave him the opportunity to demonstrate his talents as a speaker.

During this period the Treaty of Versailles was signed. Like many – perhaps most – Germans, Hitler regarded the terms of the treaty, which involved wholesale loss of land and £7,000 million in reparations, as a scandal. It was to provide an excellent focus for German resentment for many years and undoubtedly helped Hitler in his quest for power.

After completing his political training course, Hitler was asked by the army to become an intelligence officer. His role was both to gather information on subversive or potentially subversive movements and also to promote the growth of nationalist and anti-Communist ideas among soldiers. Hitler, who had never done a day's work in his life till the First World War, except for a brief spell on a building site, was now, instead of gloomily wondering how to cope with life as a demobbed soldier, being offered a paid job with a role which seemed to him glamorous and important. Before long, it was to lead to the most momentous meeting of his life.

Acting on instructions from German military intelligence, Hitler attended a meeting of the tiny German Workers Party. This had been founded in November 1918 by members of the Thule Society. The two main figures in it were Karl Harrer, a Thulist and sports writer for an evening newspaper, and Anton Drexler, a railway engineer.

In spite of its title, the German Workers Party was anything but Communist: the party programme was a mixture of nationalist and socialist ideas, with the former predominating. Hitler attended the meeting in civilian clothes and listened to a lecture on capitalism. During the discussion which followed, one member of the audience argued strongly in favour of Bavaria separating itself from Germany and uniting with Austria to form a new south German state. Hitler was incensed at these ideas and stormed out of the meeting after denouncing the whole idea of secession from Germany and losing his temper with the speaker in the process.

Drexler, the party leader, hurried after Hitler. He was impressed by both Hitler's views and the forceful way in which he argued for them. He presented Hitler with a copy of his autobiography, *My Political Awakening*, and took down his name and address. Next day Hitler received a membership card in the post and an invitation to join the party's committee. After reading Drexler's booklet, he was sufficiently impressed to sign up as a member. Drexler put him in charge of propaganda.

Hitler remained on the army payroll for another seven months, but in fact he became more or less a full-time politician.

Eckart, Harrer and Drexler were already members of the occult-racial Thule society, and with them as presiding spirits over the embryonic German Workers Party, it was hardly surprising that its inner council were steeped in occultism. This tendency was not diminished by Hitler's membership of the Party; if anything, it was strengthened. But Hitler, while as preoccupied with occultism as any on the inner council, was far more realistic about his objectives and methods than the rest of the party leadership. Hitler wanted an occult-political Reich, not simply an occult one. Before long he had become the star speaker for the party and its dominating character.

Hitler's main topics were nationalism, anti-Semitism, communism and capitalism. In all these areas he showed a strong tinge of occultism, but not so obviously as the other Thulists. For instance, he had an associate who believed that the swing of a pendulum suspended on a thread would give him the power to detect Jews.[6] This particular individual was not only an amateur astrologer but also a practising doctor.

Joseph Greiner, another who knew Hitler during his years in Vienna, tells an interesting story about his studies and activities in this period. He says that Hitler was fascinated by yogis and fakirs. On one occasion he held his hand in the flame of a burning gas jet to show the strength of his will. Hitler also attended a number of occult lectures in Vienna, which led to a fascination with movement of objects from a distance by psychic means (psychokinesis), water divining, astrology, graphology, numerology and physiognomy. Significantly, Hitler was also fascinated by, and a keen student of, hypnosis.[7]

During the very early days of Hitler's membership of the German Workers Party, when Drexler and Harrer were still the directing forces in the movement, Hitler and Harrer disagreed over party organization. Harrer, the Thule member, wanted the party to be structured like a secret occult society. Hitler, while sharing Harrer's occult interests, was anxious to make the party a real force in politics. The type of fraternity which the Thule Society was advocating would not have turned the Nazi Party into a mass movement. Hitler knew this, and argued against Harrer's position strongly. The result was that Hitler carried the day; and before long Harrer was out of the movement altogether. This marked a decisive turning-point, not only in the fortunes of the party, but also in world history. Few people, however, could have foreseen that so apparently small a step would have such devastating results for the rest of the world, effects that spread out like ripples over the next twenty-five years. For now, though it was simply another example of the legendary willpower of Hitler overcoming all opposition – even when, as in this case, it was opposition from within his own ranks.

One of the most disturbing aspects of German society in the period immediately following the First World War was the way in which at least some units of the German Army became politicized. In Bavaria this was particularly true. The 7th Army District Command engaged in undercover political activity of the most blatant kind. Among the most flagrant violations of their neutrality were: the equipping of the *Freikorps* from German army supplies; the deliberate and systematic intimidation of Liberal, Socialist and Communist supporters; and even the carrying-out of cold-blooded acts of political assassination. Among the men they murdered were Matthias Erzberger, the man who signed the Armistice and the Jewish foreign minister, Walther Rathenau, who had been an outstandingly effective minister for war during World War I. When even the murder of the foreign minister could go unpunished, it was clear to everyone that law and order had almost completely broken down in Germany.

Into this atmosphere of violence and murder stepped Hitler. Before long he had attracted the attention of Captain Ernst Röhm.

An excellent soldier and a man of tremendous energy and willpower, Röhm loved war and wept when Germany signed the Armistice. He equipped and trained a private army of some 10,000 men in addition to his own army command. Röhm hated civilians and thought that war brought out the best in men. Not surprisingly, he worked as hard as he could for the overthrow of the Social Democratic government.

Röhm became the liaison officer between the Bavarian army and the *Freikorps*. He was very impressed with Hitler and joined the Nazis soon after Hitler himself. Röhm also diverted funds from the Bavarian army to enable the Nazis to purchase their own newspaper. Although he looked on Hitler as a fine speaker and 'drummer' for the nationalist programme, he was one of the few close associates of Hitler who did not become completely dominated by him. Röhm always felt able to disagree with Hitler when he felt that his friend had stepped out of line.

In many ways, Hitler owed his success to Röhm more than to any other individual. Probably even Hitler, though, never thought that one day the captain's loyalty would be rewarded by murder on the future dictator's orders. Certainly Röhm had no idea of the depths of treachery to which the man he considered a personal friend was capable of sinking.

Röhm not only organized the financial backing for the party from army funds; he also recruited members of the *Freikorps* and even undercover regular soldiers to act as 'minders' for the Nazis. As well as the Bavarian army, many members of the Bavarian Government and the Munich police force were also supporters of, or at least sympathetic towards, the Nazi Party.

Eckart, Röhm and of course Hitler were almost entirely responsible for the phenomenal success of the party in its early days. Both Röhm and Eckart knew that the organization had political potential, if only the right man could be found to lead it. Unlike Eckart, however, Röhm was never entirely convinced that Hitler was the right man for the job.

Unlike Röhm, Eckart was looking not simply for a political

leader, but a German messiah to restore his nation's greatness and to spearhead a spiritual sea-change within the country. Unfortunately, Eckart's peculiar version of spirituality meant substituting black magic and Satanism for the more attractive manifestations of spirituality.

Before his discovery of Hitler, Eckart had been holding a whole series of seances with two anti-Semitic Russians, who were former generals. Their object was to find a new German messiah. The medium chosen was a peasant woman who managed to produce ghostly apparitions from her vagina. She also managed to hold forth in foreign languages at great length, in spite of having no knowledge of them.[8]

Eckart's co-conspirator Alfred Rosenberg, who will also feature in our story, used the seances to invoke the Beast of the Book of Revelation. During one session it was predicted that the next owner of the Spear of Destiny would be the new leader of Germany. The Spear of Destiny, said to be the spear which pierced the side of Christ, was held in the Habsburg Treasure House at Vienna and venerated as an object of deep historical and occult significance. It was also foretold that the holder of the spear would lead his country into a bloody war and would raise Germany to a position of power from which she would be abruptly cast down. This messiah was 'hard by the door', and named as Hitler.[9] However hard that may be to believe, there is an even more incredible prophecy concerning Hitler. This was actually written down in 1916 by the former German Army commander, von Moltke. He actually named Hitler in a state of trance as the future leader of Germany. At the time he was simply an insignificant and totally unknown soldier on the Western Front. He also predicted that Chamberlain – whom we shall meet in the next chapter – would be the first man openly to hail Hitler as the new German leader.[10]

Even from the early years of his life, Hitler and his few associates were all steeped in occultism. It is not too much to say that the roots of Hitler's later excursions into magical politics – which came to dominate even his military planning during the war, as we shall see in due course – were sown in his early youth.

2 The Spear of Destiny

In 1908, when Hitler was struggling with poverty in Vienna, he made a discovery which was to change his whole life and set his mind wandering along the road to conquest and world war.

Hitler spent his time in Vienna visiting museums, art galleries, libraries and going to the opera. He would live for days on bread and milk simply so that he could listen to the music of Wagner or buy occult books. One day he was in the Habsburg Treasure House and caught sight of the Spear of Destiny. Lost in thought, he suddenly heard a voice addressing a party of tourists. The guide said, 'There is a legend associated with this spear, that whoever claims it, and solves its secrets, holds the destiny of the world in his hands, for good or evil.'

Fascinated by the guide's words, Hitler focused his attention on the rest of his lecture. He heard how legend had it that this artefact was believed to be the very spear which had once pierced the side of Christ as he hung upon the cross at Calvary. In fact, as the guide explained, it could be traced back only as far as the tenth-century Emperor Otto the Great; and the nail, which was fastened within its blade, had been added some time during the thirteenth century.

While the rest of the party moved on to other exhibits, Hitler stayed behind, his eyes fixed in rapture upon the spear. What was the message it held for him? He pondered the meaning of the guide's prophecy ... *whoever claims it, and solves its secrets, holds the destiny of the world in his hands, for good or evil.*

Not knowing what the answer was, but determined to discovery it, Hitler went the next day to the Hof Library to study the weapon's history. He soon found out that, as well as the one contained in the Treasure House, there was a whole set of other spears, each of which had, at some time or other, been put forward as the actual spear which pierced Christ's side. At first this threw Hitler; but, with grim determination, he set to work to discover which of them was authentic. It seemed there was one spear, dating back to the third century, which had been traced down through the centuries until its last mention during the reign of Henry the Fowler, father of Otto the Great. Hitler was convinced that this was the same spear as the one in the Treasure House. He felt sure that he could bridge the gap between the two, and prove that they were the same spear, handed down from father to son.

In fact, neither Hitler himself nor the Ahnenerbe, the Occult Bureau which the Nazis established when they came to power in Germany, ever did succeed in making a link between the spears. However, a man who will figure prominently in this chapter, Dr Walter Stein, discovered that Henry the Fowler had sent the spear to King Athelstan of England, who had used it to defeat the Danes at the Battle of Malmesbury (c. 926-27). When Henry's son Otto the Great married the sister of Athelstan, the English king presented it to Otto as a wedding gift. But of this part of the spear's history, Hitler was to remain forever unaware.

Although he never did prove the connection, Hitler did manage to uncover enough facts to convince him that his intuition was correct. The spear which stood in the Habsburg Treasure House was indeed the Spear of Destiny. Throughout the centuries it had been associated with many men of destiny. The Roman emperor Constantine the Great, the first Christian emperor, carried the spear to the Battle of the Milvian Bridge, where he overcame Maxentius, his rival claimant for the Empire. He also held the spear in his hands at the notorious council of Nicaea, when, in one of the first tastes of the future of Christianity, Constantine forced his own version of the religion upon the rest of the empire, and introduced the dogma of the Trinity. This led to centuries of dissension within the Church and laid the foundations for many of the subsequent Christian persecutions of other religions and other brands of Christianity. When the emperor, now an old man, built Constantinople to be the new Rome, he carried the spear with him when he was drawing the boundaries of the new city.

Other men of destiny who had owned the spear were Alaric the

Goth, who sacked Rome; Aetius, the last man successfully to hold together the Roman Empire in the West; Justinian, the codifier of Roman Law; Charles Martel, the ruler (but not king) of the Franks, who drove back an invading Arab army from France while holding the spear. Charlemagne too had possessed the spear and used it to found his own empire. Through Charlemagne the spear passed into the hands of the Holy Roman emperors.

Of all the Holy Roman emperors, the most remarkable were members of the Hohenstaufen dynasty. These included the famous Frederick Barbarossa and his grandson Frederick II, whose nickname was '*Stupor Mundi*', 'the Wonder of the World'. Frederick II was not only the finest military genius of his age, but also a man of high culture. He was the patron of the Minnesingers, the German equivalent of the Troubadours. In addition, he was a poet and musician of no mean gifts, and a man 'so various, that he seem'd to be Not one, but all Mankind's Epitome'.[1] He was a speaker of six languages, one of the most chivalrous knights of his time and also one of the most cynical politicians. Frederick was a man so charismatic that even popes were abashed in his presence. He was also a master of occult powers. Among his many occult acquaintances were the leader of the notorious Assassins, whose combination of occult learning and political murder terrorized the Middle East for two centuries. Frederick also had his own harem, practised astrology and made many experiments in alchemy. He carried the spear with him on the Sixth Crusade, one of the few crusades to be successful in recovering Jerusalem.

Even more important to Hitler than the deeds of valour which his hero Frederick II had performed, however, was the fact that the spear had been the catalyst for the foundation of the Teutonic Knights, of whose chivalric order the SS was later to become the black and bloody caricature.

For three whole days after his discovery of the Spear of Destiny, Hitler studied its history in the library. During the course of his reading, he also took a liking to the windy nonsense of Hegel's so-called philosophy. From Hegel he took an authoritarian conception of the state and the even more sinister idea that what Hegel called 'heroes who carry out the will of the world spirit' could do no wrong, and had the absolute and unqualified right to destroy anything and anyone who stood in their way. He knew that it was the spear which held the key to unlock his own destiny as a German hero. How could he turn its power to his own account, to raise his own country and all Germans to a realization and fulfilment of their high historic destiny?

Later, on the afternoon of the fourth day, Hitler went back to the Habsburg Treasure House to gaze again upon the Spear of Destiny. Over the next three years he was to make this selfsame journey again and again, seeking to wrest from the ancient spear its historic secrets. On this particular evening, three days after he had first laid eyes upon the artefact, Hitler was standing in the Treasure House. He felt strange power coming from the spear, but did not know what it was. Baffled, he stood before it, gazing at the ancient relic. Slowly, painfully, he stood there, trying to piece together the story of the spear. As he gazed in rapture upon the holy lance, Hitler went into a state of trance. In his own words, 'I slowly became aware of a mighty presence around it – the same awesome presence which I had experienced inwardly on those rare occasions in my life when I had sensed that a great destiny awaited me.'[2]

So it was that, after painful searching for the truth, Hitler awoke suddenly to a blinding insight. The spear, he realized, was more than a simple object: rather, it was, in Hitler's own words, 'a bridge between the world of sense and the world of the spirit'. He also claimed that it was at this very moment in time that he grasped his own part in the future history of the world. As he put it, 'A window in the future was opened up to me through which I saw in a single flash of illumination a future event by which I knew beyond contradiction that the blood in my veins would one day become the vessel of the Folk-Spirit of my people.'[3]

In a strange state of mystical exaltation, and for one of the few times in his life truly humble, Hitler left the Treasure House at last. His faltering footsteps took him back into the world of poverty and squalor which was the everyday reality of his life. But in his heart, he was on fire with a dream of destiny. In that moment he knew in his heart that he, Adolf Hitler, would one day become the proud owner of the Spear of Destiny, and with it carve out a lasting place in world history. That very night he left the Vienna lodgings which he had shared with his friend Kubizek. When, a little later, the music student returned from holiday, he found his friend gone. He never saw him again. 'Whatever could have made Adolf Hitler leave me without a word or a sign?' Kubizek asked himself in astonishment. Though in many ways he had found Hitler demanding, he did admit in his own record of their youthful association, written years later when his friend had become the ruler of Germany, that in comparison with the time he had spent with Hitler, the rest of his life had seemed flat and empty.

Hitler spent the next three years living in a series of Vienna doss-houses. He fed himself at soup kitchens, dressed so shabbily that he looked like a tramp, and spent his time in libraries, art galleries, at the opera and the Habsburg Treasure House. He was beginning to acquire a reputation as a shiftless, lazy sponger. But the opinions of others did not concern him in the least. He knew that he was a man favoured by providence. It was while he was still brooding on how to unlock the powers of the spear and turn them to his own use that he came upon Wagner's opera *Parsifal*. Sitting in the cheap seats at the Vienna Opera, Hitler listened to the music, enthralled. He was excited by the ceremony of the grail and the haunting melody of the music, but disgusted by the grail knights' vows of renunciation, humility and compassion. 'I could find no cause for admiration for the piddling Knights who had dishonoured their Aryan blood to follow the superstitions of the Jew, Jesus. My sympathy was entirely with Klingsor.'

One can see already, in Hitler's preference for the sexual pervert and political tyrant Klingsor, the roots of the ideology which was later to issue in the death camps of Auschwitz and Treblinka and the rest of the gallery of horrors we know from the Nazi regime. Even at the age of nineteen Hitler had already taken a conscious decision to choose evil over good.

Hitler's researches into the spear soon uncovered the fact that it was the same inspiration which had led Wagner to compose *Parsifal*. Wagner too had spent much time studying the Spear of Destiny in the Habsburg Treasure House, while working out the plan of his opera in his mind.

Hitler was now faced with a further dilemma: Wagner and Nietzsche were his two idols, and yet here was the composer promulgating the Christian virtues of humility and compassion and the philosopher denouncing these same virtues and *Parsifal* itself as a sick denial of life. Many people might feel that these two points of view were irreconcilable; but not Hitler. He promptly decided that the grail could still be a proper source of inspiration for a German, provided that it was accorded a pagan interpretation. At the same time he agreed with Nietzsche about Christianity and what both men saw as the loathsome sentimentality of the grail knights. Instead of chivalry and compassion, Hitler wanted to substitute courage and strength, endurance and willpower. He also made his own highly distorted interpretation of Nietzsche's 'transvaluation of all values'. Instead of the subtle and intricate structure of Nietzsche's thought, Hitler simply stood Christianity on its head and decided that whatever Christ called evil was good, and whatever he called good was evil. Thus love, forgiveness, trust and all the other kindlier virtues held no place in Hitler's heart. Only the harsher virtues remained, together with a viper's nest of poisonous vices masquerading as goodness. Having taken this decision, he went and stood before the spear which even he believed had pierced the side of Christ, and swore to make evil his good.

At this point Hitler was almost overcome with emotion. In his own words, 'The noisy scene of the Treasure House seemed to melt away before my eyes. I stood alone and trembling before the hovering form of the Superman – a Spirit sublime and fearful, a countenance intrepid and cruel. I offered my soul as a vessel of his Will.'[4] That Hitler could have found it possible, let alone desirable, to worship a being whom he himself called 'intrepid and cruel' shows more adequately than any commentary how muddy his soul had already become. But for many years yet he had no opportunity to show how evil he had already become.

At this point in the story an enigmatic and enlightened figure enters our story: Dr Walter Johannes Stein. We have already briefly referred to Stein once. Now we must look at his account of how he came to meet Hitler in Vienna.

At the time of their meeting Stein was undergraduate at university. He was studying for a science degree, but one of the compulsory subjects at Vienna University was a brief course on

German Literature. One of the books on this course was *Parsifal*. Stein's fascination with the story, and in particular with its implications for the world, led to years of research into the grail legends. He set out to answer the questions which had baffled experts in the field for centuries. What was the grail, and why do different legends speak of it as if it were different things? Many legends refer to it as a cup, others as a stone; still others as if it were a psychological experience. And in the Arthurian legends the grail is always referred to as holy, yet *Parsifal* never once terms it thus. Why this strange omission? Stein also wondered if the material in the grail cycle was simply legendary, or allegorical, or whether it had some basis in historical fact.

While he was pondering on these questions, Stein went to see a performance of Wagner's *Parsifal*. This made him very excited, not only because of the quality of the opera but because, for the first time, Stein thought he saw a glimmer of light which might help him in his researches. The spear of which Wagner had written, Stein soon discovered, actually existed, and Wagner himself had drawn inspiration from viewing it in the Habsburg Treasure House. Before long Stein had not only seen the spear for himself but had also spent many months researching its history in the Hofburg Library in Vienna. Even Stein himself probably never guessed that his researches into the spear and the grail would occupy more than twenty years of his life.

Before long Stein had come to the conclusion that the grail stories were no mere legends, but a veiled account of real events and real people during the ninth century.[5] Charlemagne had raised the kingdom of the Franks to a point at which he was actually crowned Holy Roman emperor by the pope, placing his rule on an equal footing with the emperor at Constantinople. For a time, indeed, men once again spoke of the Roman Empire in the West, to distinguish it from its counterpart in the East. And the achievements of Charlemagne were considerable. He not only established his Empire as a first-class military power, but also began the slow revival of learning which was to culminate eventually in the Renaissance.

The Carolingian dynasty (AD 751–987) headed by Charle-magne, was preceded by the Merovingians, who were deposed by the future emperor's father, Pepin the Short, when he made himself king. The Merovingians had made the Tribal Spear their emblem, but Charlemagne instead substituted the Spear of Destiny. To him it was a symbol of Christ's blood and he used the spear to begin the whole theory of the divine right of kings. With military strength, the revival of learning and the growth of cities and trade, his empire looked to have a bright future.

In fact, however, this promise was not to be fulfilled. Charlemagne's son and successor was a weak and incompetent ruler, and when he in his turn died the vast Empire that Charlemagne had built fell apart. The Vikings became a major political and military factor at this time, and the foundation of a western empire led to the growing split in Christendom between the Byzantine and Roman Churches. For all the genius of Charlemagne, he could not prevent the next hundred years being a time of darkness and destruction.

As Stein pursued his researches into the grail, Stein had no idea of what an astonishing future Hitler was to have, and how much evil and suffering he would unleash upon the world in his pursuit of power and black magic. One day Stein went out walking in the city of Vienna, in search of some occult bookshops which he hoped might be able to help him in his researches.

In a dark and dingy shop bearing the name of Ernst Pretzsche, Stein made the discovery which was to change his whole life. From among the many volumes that lay on the shelves, he picked up and began to read a copy of *Parsifal*. But this was not any edition of the poem. As he read the book, Stein found time and again countless annotations in the same hand – notes which displayed an astonishingly profound occult learning. It was clear to Stein that the writer of the notes had also stumbled on to the fact that the poem referred to personalities and events of the ninth century. On impulse, Stein bought the book and walked through the streets of the city to a café which he sometimes frequented.

As he sat at his table reading, Stein became aware that the writer of the notes possessed not only a deep occult learning but also suffered from pathological racism. What was more, it was also clear that the writer had delved deeply into black magic. The writer's ability to unravel the mysteries of the grail impressed him deeply; yet he clearly rejected the Christian message of the poem and preferred to side with the forces of evil. For instance, a note which referred to the knights of the grail castle, made Stein shudder: 'These men betrayed their pure Aryan Blood to the dirty superstitions of the Jew Jesus – superstitions as loathsome and ludicrous as the Yiddish rites of circumcision.'

Again and again the writer of the notes gave proof of his deep occult learning. He seemed to be versed in alchemy, astrology, the classics, mythology, mysticism, yoga and oriental religions. He also wrote in a scholarly fashion about the history of the period – one of the least well known of the Middle Ages.

In *Parsifal*, the grail is described as *Lapsis Excellis*, which means 'precious stone'. A footnote by the annotator claimed that this stone was an alchemical code for the pineal gland, or third eye. And the note went on to claim that the grail story described an initiation cycle which was intended to open the third eye of the magical adept.

Many of the characters in both the poem and Wagner's opera were identified as historical people. The most important of these identifications was that of Klingsor, the black magician, with Landulf of Capua, the most sinister figure of his time. What was more, the struggle between the grail knights and Klingsor was said to be for the possession of the actual Spear of Destiny.

This discovery of Klingsor's real identity astounded Stein, for he had come across Landulf in his own researches. And what he had found out was horrifying. Landulf had practised the most appalling rites of black magic, involving not only sexual perversions but even human sacrifice. And this was the man with whom the unknown writer of the notes was identifying Klingsor, and clearly admiringly.

As he read in a mixture of astonishment and disgust, Stein suddenly became aware of a dark, malevolent presence forcing its way into his mind. Dismissing it as mere imagination, the result of having become too emotionally involved with his material, he continued to study the notes.

But the uncomfortable feeling of malevolence refused to leave him. Looking up from the book in puzzled irritation, Stein glanced through the window of the café and saw a short man, dressed in shabby clothes, hair in confusion, a tiny beard and a ridiculous-looking moustache. But the face of the man, and especially his eyes, were not at all in accordance with his appearance. Stein saw there the arrogance of one whose heart was full of contempt for his fellow men, and in the eyes he saw a brooding, hypnotic power. The man was trying to sell water-colours to passers-by in the street.

Getting up to leave the café, Stein bought three of the artist's paintings. He felt sorry for the man and did not even look at the pictures until he got home. Then he realized that one of them depicted the Spear of Destiny in the Treasure House. But what shook him rigid was that the artist's signature on the back of the painting was the same as that on the copy of *Parsifal* he had bought that day: Adolf Hitler.[6]

Stein felt that this occurrence was too strange to be put down to mere coincidence. Surely what Jung termed by the somewhat pompous name of 'synchronicity' was at work here? Somehow his destiny and that of the penniless painter were linked together inextricably, for good or evil. At all costs he must find and speak with Hitler. But this did not turn out to be an easy task. When a man wishes to lose himself in a large city, particularly when he is known to nobody, it is an easy enough matter. But when that man is also a master of black magic, it becomes easier still. So it was that Stein searched and searched in vain for the evil genius who had penned the notes on *Parsifal*.

Naturally he returned at once to the café where he had first caught sight of that demonic face. He explored all the usual tourist sights, hoping to find Hitler there painting some more of his water-colours. But it was only when, as a last resort, he returned to the shop from which he had purchased Hitler's copy of *Parsifal* that he finally struck gold.

As soon as Stein mentioned Hitler's name, the bookseller showed immediate interest. Calling him into the office at the rear of the shop, he invited Stein to sit. Hitler was apparently a frequent customer of the shop. He came in and talked with the proprietor often. Although he had not been seen there lately ...

Pretzsche, the bookshop owner, pointed to a pile in the corner of the office and complained that Hitler scribbled furiously on all his books. The volume of *Parsifal* had been sold to Stein by mistake, since normally the shop never put Hitler's books on sale. The impoverished painter used to come to his shop and pawn his books to buy food.

Stein was fascinated by the pile of books the shopkeeper had indicated. He knew that what books a man owns provides a great insight into his mind. He saw several philosophical works: Hegel, Nietzsche, Fichte, Schelling and Schopenhauer. Ironically, Schopenhauer would have been disgusted at the company he was keeping. And he would have disapproved even more strongly of the racist ramblings of Chamberlain, whose work, *The Foundations of the Nineteenth Century*, was also in Pretzsche's office, and who plays a key role in the events of this book. Goethe, that great representative of the spirit of German enlightenment and humanitarian ideals, was there too. Equally incongruous was a book on Jewish culture by Lessing. The rest of the heap consisted of works on German mythology, oriental religions and textbooks on yoga.

Together with the books, a large number of water-colours by Hitler were displayed in the office. Clearly, Pretzsche had been giving considerable financial help to the young painter. Stein also recognized a group photograph which included the notorious Guido von List, a black magician recently involved in a scandal, and who was pictured standing next to the bookshop owner.

Pretzsche had the audacity to tell Stein that he was a great authority on occult matters and that it would be perfectly all right for the young student to ask his advice and instruction in them, which he was already giving freely to other young men, including Hitler. But Stein felt no desire to prolong his acquaintance with the bookseller. He felt an inward disgust towards Pretzsche and was anxious to get away. But he still had to get what he had come for: Hitler's address. Pretzsche gave it to Stein and he left gladly, anxious to be free of the stifling presence of evil he had felt inside that room.

The young doctor Stein decided to go and visit Hitler at the hostel which Pretzsche had given as his current address. But to his surprise it seemed that Hitler was no longer there. Apparently an aunt of his had just died and left him some money. It was possible that he would return to the hostel.

There followed a rather puzzling episode. According to Stein his first meeting with Hitler took place in the summer of 1912. Yet it was March 1911 when the aunt died and left Hitler a legacy. Is it really likely that Hitler would have waited until the summer of 1912 to collect the money from her estate? –

especially considering the general poverty in which he had been living. What seems more probable is that Stein's memory was at fault when, many years later, he described the circumstances of their first meeting.[7]

When Stein did come face to face with Hitler it was after he had received his legacy. The shabby, unkempt figure he had seen through the windows of the café had been transformed into what another acquaintance of Hitler's called, 'a local tax-collector in his Sunday best'. Gone was the beard and straggling mass of hair; gone too the clothes which had once been so verminous that the authorities at the doss-house where Hitler stayed had forcibly removed them for delousing. He was still in possession of the tiny clipped moustache and the forelock of brown hair which hung over his forehead; but his appearance had been radically improved. He wore a suit and a clean shirt, and had even managed to buy himself a new pair of shoes. So different did he look now that at first Stein had trouble recognizing the poverty-stricken painter he had seen before.

At the time Stein saw him again Hitler was painting a large picture of the Ring of the Nibelungs, a key object in Germany's national epic poem, *'Das Nibelungenlied*, which, in turn, was the basis for Wagner's celebrated operatic cycle. Thinking to get off on the right foot, Stein made the usual conventional noises about admiration for the work in progress. Much to his surprise, Hitler was irritated with him for disturbing him while he was working. And when Stein, in an effort to pacify him, produced the annotated *Parsifal* Hitler flew into a fury. He denounced Pretzsche for daring to sell his book and Stein for presuming to contact him. It seemed as if their meeting was about to come to an unpleasant end when Stein, in desperation, came right to the point. He had been researching into the grail legends, and had come across Hitler's notes in the copy of *Parsifal* he had bought in the bookshop. He had been immediately impressed by the obviously deep occult and historical learning conveyed in them. What was more – he baited the hook – he had discovered that the Roman centurion Longinus – who was said to have been the soldier whose spear pierced Christ's side – was in fact German.

This made Hitler take notice of Stein at last. In fact, he became positively effusive. The two men spent the next hour discussing the history of the spear and the strange destiny which it always seemed to bring to the man who owned it. In a state of high excitement, the two of them went straight away to the Treasure House to see the spear once more. As the two of them stood in silence before the ancient relic, both men seemed overcome with emotion.

Stein stood lost in wonder and humility, feeling as if at that moment the very scenes of Christ's crucifixion were being re-enacted before his own eyes. He felt a strong healing power flowing into him from the spear, a deep sense of love and compassion. Transported into a state of ecstasy, he completely forgot that he was not alone. Returning to everyday waking consciousness at last, he came to himself with a start and looked around him anxiously. But he had no need to worry. Hitler too was sunk deeply into a trance of his own. He was literally swaying to and fro as he stood there. Stein gazed in horror at him, wondering what evil responses the spear was evoking in Hitler's twisted brain. Struck by the apparition, Stein actually wondered for a moment if Hitler's soul had become for a moment the living embodiment of the Antichrist.

Over a period of time Stein got to know Hitler quite well. He saw him changing and growing more self-confident. Stein even had some hope that he might be able to humanize Hitler. On this, however, he was sadly mistaken. Instead it was Hitler who tried to convert Stein to the viewpoint of German racism. Stein was fascinated by Hitler, not only because of his occult learning but also the sheer mesmeric force of his personality, which at times threatened to overpower even the most hostile listener. Hitler would pick political arguments with perfect strangers and Stein cringed in embarrassment whenever he did this in his company.

The grail stories, Hitler explained to Stein, described the process of initiation into magical wisdom. He demonstrated how each symbol corresponded to an initiatory degree. The grail had no real connection with Christianity, commentators having deliberately distorted its meaning to put it into a Christian framework.

Stein was wondering how such men as Pretzsche and von List had become involved with Hitler. As the latter became gradually more communicative, he eventually explained this to Stein. Pretzsche had been impressed by Hitler when he talked with him in his bookshop, and after several meetings Pretzsche started teaching Hitler some basic occultism. As time went on he initiated Hitler into the arts of black magic and also got him to take hallucinogenic drugs to 'expand our consciousness'.[8] The results were far above Hitler's expectations. He seemed to make contact with a reality different from that which lay around him, a world with a different vision, a harsher morality. One recalls a passage from *Mein Kampf* where Hitler preaches this degraded conception of morality. The passage in question runs: 'It is not by the principles of humanity that man lives by or is able to preserve himself above the animal world but solely by means of the most brutal struggle.' This is social Darwinism with a vengeance! Compassion, sensitivity, love of life – all are discarded in this outlook as useless. All that remains is the will to live alone, the mere animal instinct for survival. Surely, Stein protested when Hitler said such things, there must be more to life than that, some purpose, some meaning? But Hitler would have none of it. To him, that kind of talk was silly sentimentality, a decaying remnant of the corruptions of Christianity.

The last time the two men met was just after the future leader of Germany had been to see Wagner's opera *The Meistersingers*. He was full of praise for the work and also highly pleased with himself. Hitler told Stein that he was leaving Vienna soon and going to live in Munich and that he was busily engaged in trying to discover his previous reincarnations. He wondered openly if he had been Frederick Barbarossa, or Alaric, or some great German hero from the past. But now, after his programme of magical training, he had discovered the truth. In one of his previous incarnations, Hitler told an incredulous Stein, he had been Landulf of Capua, the historical original of Klingsor, the black magician in the grail legends. Far from being some hero, Hitler believed himself to be what Stein later called 'the chalice for the Spirit of the Anti-Christ'![9]

After this last meeting Hitler left Vienna and never saw Stein again. In spite of Hitler's insistence that he was going to Munich, this seems to have simply been a lie. We have already argued that Stein's meetings with Hitler took place not between 1912 and 1913, but between 1911 and 1912. It is true that Hitler went to Munich in 1913; it is also true that Hitler claimed to have gone there in 1912. And yet it seems certain that he did not do so. But if Stein saw Hitler for the last time in 1912, not 1913, suddenly Hitler's activities start to make sense. For since 1909 Hitler had been moving from one disreputable doss-house to another in an effort to avoid conscription into the Austrian army. And we have the testimony of his own sister-in-law that Hitler came to Liverpool in 1912 and stayed with her family for some time.[10] When he left Liverpool he came to Germany and settled in Munich. Although eventually the Austrian authorities tracked him down there, as we have seen, he was able to spin them a convincing yarn and was rejected as medically unfit. In the light of Hitler's subsequent career, one wonders if the medical grounds for refusal were mental rather than physical.

3 The Nazis and Astrology

Goering is worried about the stars on his chest, Himmler about
those in his horoscope.[1]

As might be expected from a movement whose origins were
steeped in occultism, the Nazi leadership was obsessed with all
kinds of predictive practices. Astrology, of course, is one of the
oldest of these, and relatively speaking one of the more
respectable. The two basic divisions of the art are natal
astrology, which deals with the horoscopes of individuals, and
mundane astrology, which studies the horoscopes of nations.
Although natal astrology was to play an important part in the
Nazis' occult involvement over the years, they were even more
interested in mundane astrology. With an obsessional eagerness
they pored over charts of planets and stars, looking desperately
for signs of German victories.

An occultist who enters our story at this point is a woman
called Elsbeth Ebertin, whose involvement with the Nazis was to
make her famous. Not long after the spring of 1923, before
Hitler had attempted his failed *putsch* which was to make him a
national celebrity, this graphologist and astrologer received a
letter from a woman who was a keen Nazi. In the letter she was
given the date and place of Hitler's birth, but not the time.
Without the time of birth, it is, of course, impossible to cast a
correct horoscope. There are two basic ways of getting round
this problem. One is to draw up what is known as a 'Hindu
chart', which uses the time of sunrise on the date of birth. The
other is to use a process known as 'rectification'. In this more
popular method, charts are drawn for various likely moments of

birth. These are then compared with what the astrologer knows of the subject's life and character, and one is selected as the most likely. This is what Ebertin, without a great deal of information to go on, did.

In fact, her estimate of the time of birth based on rectification was entirely wrong. But in spite of this, Ebertin erected a chart for Hitler on the basis of it, and when she published it in 1924 it created a sensation. She described Hitler as 'a man of action', who 'can expose himself to personal danger by reckless action'. His stars showed that he was a natural leader, 'fated to sacrifice himself for the German nation and to face up to all circumstances with audacity and courage, even when it is a matter of life and death, and to give an impulse to a German freedom movement.'

Ebertin was so struck with the glorious destiny which she foresaw for Hitler that in late 1923 she actually moved to Munich to watch the development of his career. She went to hear his speeches and once even conversed with him directly. Ebertin's impression of Hitler was that on a one-to-one basis he was 'rather shy', and only came out of himself when he was facing a large crowd. Then he could become positively hypnotic. 'On the platform,' she said, 'he is like a man possessed.' Hitler's trial and imprisonment, she predicted, would not only benefit his movement, but also give 'a massive impetus to the pendulum of world history'.[2]

Ebertin's prediction made her overnight the most famous astrologer in Germany. She came to be in constant demand. It also made people aware, often for the first time, of the links between Hitler and occultism, at least in the field of astrology. Nor was her prediction without influence on Hitler himself. Even after the Nazis had achieved power, when they immediately began to suppress astrology and occultism in general, Ebertin, though the best-known astrologer in Germany, was left alone and allowed to continue with her work. This is particularly surprising in view of the fact that the Nazis made it a criminal offence to publish or even cast a horoscope of Hitler. The only possible explanation is that Hitler himself gave orders for her not to be molested. Certainly he referred to Ebertin's prediction many times in his life and in terms which suggested it had done him a power of good. Hitler was clearly grateful to her for having published her revelations at such a crucial period in his career.

After the German elections of 1930 the Nazis for the first time became a mass movement. At this point Hitler began to distance himself from the *völkisch* occultists who had been his constant companions for years. Erich Hanussen was one psychic and astrologer who at first enjoyed great influence within the party. In time, though, his ability accurately to describe and predict the Nazis' secret projects led to his being considered too dangerous to live. His assassination was duly organized as a security measure![3]

When the Nazis finally took power in 1933 many occultists hoped for a state of affairs in which they could enjoy great influence. They could not have been more tragically mistaken. To a large extent this was due to the fact that the first Nazi government was a coalition of unlikely allies, which might fall at any time. It was essential for Hitler that the party should distance itself from the murkier aspects of its own past. The last thing the Nazi leaders wanted was for the extent of their involvement in black magic and Satanism to become generally known.

Astrologers were singled out for particular persecution. The Nazis seem to have started out with the idea of taking astrology over and incorporating it within the Party, but, when it became clear this could not be done, they turned to intimidation. The leader of the Central Astrological Office, to which most German astrologers belonged, was arrested. He was accused of being Jewish and of having joined the Nazis under false pretences. Although he was soon released, he became much more cautious.[4]

The next step in the Nazi campaign was to instruct newspapers to refuse all astrological advertising. The next stage was to ban all methods of fortune-telling and astrology in Berlin. Astrological and occult literature was then banned throughout Germany. This did not at first apply to the more learned type of occult work, but the Nazis used tactics of economic intimidation to curb their sale and publication. Random raids were made by the police on all occult booksellers and publishers. All material was seized, allegedly so that it could be examined, but in fact it was never returned to its owners. After a few examples of this random confiscation of occult works, most publishers and booksellers got the message. They simply stopped producing or selling books which fell foul of the authorities. Within two years of Hitler's appointment as German Chancellor, occult literature had been all but stamped out.

In 1935 the Nazis decided to control what little amount of occult work had managed to survive the previous two years. A Nazi, known simply as Herr Schulze, who was also a keen astrologer was given the power to censor all astrological publications and to allow those which received his official seal of approval to carry on. Politically harmless occultists were also forced to join the German Labour Front, the Nazi labour organization which had replaced the old trade unions. However, this state of semi-toleration only lasted for two more years.

In 1937 the Nazis decided that occultism was too dangerous in itself to be allowed to influence the minds of the German people. A sustained campaign of propaganda, intimidation and restriction on paper supplies for occult publishers managed to all but complete the work of suppression begun four years before.[5]

Next year the Nazis conquered Austria. Even Lanz, Hitler's old mentor, who lived there, was forbidden to write, speak or publish. All occult societies were banned and their members subjected to at least psychological investigation by the Gestapo. Many were simply thrown into concentration camps and died there.

In 1939 a Swiss astrologer, Karl Krafft was to make an astonishing prediction. A keen Nazi, Krafft used to write letters to his friends displaying the usual paranoia about Jews and Freemasons. He also knew a Dr Fesel, another astrologer, who belonged to Department VII of the SS. From time to time Fesel commissioned Krafft to draw up an astrological guide to world affairs. But the report which Krafft sent to Fesel on 2 November 1939 was no ordinary horoscope. So specific and so astoundingly foolhardy from a practical point of view was this special horoscope, that it attracted the immediate attention of Goebbels himself.

Krafft told Fesel that, between 8 and 9 November 1939, Hitler's life would be in danger from 'an attempt of assassination by the use of explosive material'. On 8 November

1939, a few minutes after Hitler had left the meeting at Munich where he had been speaking, a hidden time-bomb exploded, killing seven Nazi Party members and injuring a number of others.[6]

The anniversary of Hitler's failed Munich *putsch*, 8 November, was one of the great days in the Nazi calendar. Every year Nazis came faithfully to Munich to commemorate the event, listening to a speech by Hitler and exchanging memories and conversation. It had come to assume the status of a religious pilgrimage; even those party members who had not been involved in the *putsch* turned up as a matter of course: their Messiah would speak to them again.

The Germans had grown to rapid and astonishing successes in the last three years. Hitler and his ministers had been speaking of 'the will to peace'. Now that Poland had been conquered, many Germans thought that Britain and France would make peace with their country. Even Hitler himself had been saying so openly.

But tonight it was different. Hitler turned up in more sombre mood, warning the audience that they faced the prospect of a long war. He told them that he had asked Goering to prepare for five more years of struggle. In the circumstances, this seemed a strange thing to say. Poland had been conquered and on the Western Front the war was totally non-existent. Not one shot in anger had been fired between the Germans and their opponents on the Western Front. It was the period of the so-called 'Phoney War', and in the real fighting, German arms had been everywhere victorious.

But that was not the only strange thing about that night's meeting. Contrary to his usual custom, Hitler made a very short speech and left soon afterwards. This was very odd, as he was in the habit of staying behind for hours to talk over old times with his former comrades-in-arms. Instead he left, together with his entourage, just after nine o'clock.

At 9.10 p.m. a bomb exploded in the hall, directly behind the platform. Seven people were killed, sixty-three injured, and the hall itself was devastated. The very place where Hitler had stood was buried in a mountain of debris, and had he still been in the hall, he would certainly have been killed.

Hitler heard the news of the explosion at Nuremberg, as he

was returning home on the train. The news both astonished him and left him in a state of almost mystical exaltation. Eyes blazing with excitement, he shouted, 'Now I am content! The fact that I left the Bürgerbrau earlier than usual is a corroboration of Providence's intention to allow me to reach my goal!' And, as we know, Hitler had precognitive abilities.[7]

But the November bomb plot had still further occult repercussions. For Krafft himself, who had predicted that exactly such a plot would take place, suddenly found himself under investigation by the Gestapo. And the way in which this happened displays a naivety bordering on the incredible. Krafft sent a telegram to Hess, openly boasting about the fact that he had predicted a bomb plot against Hitler's life. Not surprisingly, the Gestapo immediately interrogated the Swiss astrologer. It was with considerable difficulty that Krafft persuaded them that he had known about the plot only through the stars.

However, once he had talked his way out of a very nasty situation, Krafft's predictive abilities made him suddenly in demand with the Nazi hierarchy. For the next five years he worked for the occult propaganda machine in Germany. In spite of his loyalty to the Party, and his involvement with such activities as astrological predictions of German victories, Krafft in the end fared no better than most German astrologers. He too died in a concentration camp in 1944.

At this point a colourful character enters our story: Louis de Wohl, a refugee who was to become the official astrologer to the British Government. De Wohl was recruited after Krafft had made a prediction about Romania and its future. Not surprisingly, the Romanian Ambassador in London was very interested in this. Taking advantage of his position, he recommended de Wohl for the post of Churchill's astrologer. Since it was well known to Churchill and the British government generally that Hitler did believe in and consult astrologers, Churchill felt that de Wohl might as well be employed. The latter's job was essentially to tell Churchill what Hitler's astrologers were telling him.

This was doubly difficult. In the first place, de Wohl had actually to draw up the horoscopes and interpret them. But, in addition, he had to guess how much of what the German astrologers saw they were passing on to their masters. Given that the last thing the Nazis wanted to hear was bad news, and that the situation got worse as the war went on, it seemed likely to de Wohl that the German astrologers would therefore be very selective as regards the information they passed on. De Wohl saw Krafft as his main astrological opponent. However, as time went on his German adversary was to fall from favour. As no one outside Germany knew that Krafft had been sent to a concentration camp, De Wohl's mistake was understandable.[8]

In 1941 Hess made his famous flight to Britain, to try and conclude a separate peace. He believed (wrongly) that the Duke of Hamilton was a Nazi sympathizer who would help him to this end. The mission was undertaken by him after a dream by Haushofer and a prediction by an unknown astrologer.[9] Following Hess's flight, the Nazis set to work on yet another purge of the star-gazing fraternity. Virtually all the non-Nazi astrologers were now rounded up into concentration camps, and many of the Nazi ones too. Not until the final weeks of the war did astrology surface again in Nazi occult thinking. This time it was in the bunker at Berlin, with Hitler and Goebbels desperately looking for a way out of an impossible situation.

Goebbels was reading to Hitler about the campaigns of Frederick the Great. At one point Frederick was completely encircled by his enemies and no escape seemed in sight. Then the Tsarina died and the Russians pulled out of the war. Soon after he had read Hitler this passage, Goebbels heard the news of the death of Roosevelt.

'My Führer, I congratulate you,' said Goebbels. 'Roosevelt is dead. It is written in the stars that the second half of April will be the turning point for us. This is Friday, 13th April. It is the turning point.' Hitler's horoscope was promptly dragged out and eagerly studied for any signs of such a change of fortune. But, whatever the stars might have said, the earth around them was silent. Only the harsh music of guns serenaded the beleaguered bunker until its eventual fall.[10]

Curiously enough, both Hitler's chart and the horoscope for the German Republic predicted war in 1939, victories until 1941, then defeats up to 1945, followed by a German recovery and victory. The interesting thing is that both Hitler and Goebbels compared the charts themselves. This is no easy task, and demonstrates once again the extent to which the Nazi leaders were steeped in the techniques of astrology. Not only Hitler and Goebbels took such an interest, however. Himmler too had his own astrologer, constantly consulted by him right up to 1945.[11]

Krafft was also the founder of a discipline known as 'astro-biology', which he developed in addition to his orthodox astrological activities. He published his *Treatise on Astro-Biology* in 1939, the same year that he made his astonishing prediction about the bomb plot against Hitler. Krafft checked the birth dates of 2,800 musicians and declared that there was a close relation between their sun sign, temperament and family history. This idea was subsequently shown to be based on wishful thinking.[12] Things must have been even more difficult for Nazi astrologers than ordinary ones, since they had to take on board the entire Nazi racial mythology as well. Any astrologer who argued that a German, a Jew and a Negro who shared the same sun sign were all astrologically similar was officially rejected by the Nazis as being 'unscientific'.

Himmler's own favourite astrologer, Wulf, foresaw not only the attempt on Hitler's life in 1944 but even a sinal infection which Hitler was to develop. He also predicted a 'mysterious death' for Hitler at some time not long before 7 May 1945. Wulf also studied poisons and Sanskrit.[13]

Wulf was arrested, like other astrologers, after Hess's flight to England. However, before long he was released and became astrologer-in-chief to Himmler. As well as the three successful predictions we have already seen, Wulf foresaw that Hitler's invasion of Russia would lose him the war. He was also able, by using a Hindu astrological method, to locate the whereabouts of Mussolini after the overthrow of his government in Italy before his rescue by German troops. Himmler was greatly impressed by these and other predictions which the astrologer made. However, when Wulf prophesied a Russian invasion, citing a pamphlet which he had written called 'Is Another Mongol Invasion Imminent?', Himmler reacted violently. However, through his friendship with another man who will figure later in our work, Hitler's masseur Kersten, Wulf tried to influence Himmler into deposing Hitler and trying to make peace with the Western Allies. He also got involved in attempts to secure an end to the extermination of Jews and the release of Jewish prisoners. To some extent, Wulf and Kersten actually had some success in this, as will be seen later.

On 15 April 1945 Himmler handed the horoscopes of various Nazi leaders, particularly Speer and Bormann, to Wulf.[14] The astrologer was asked to give his opinion on their suitability for inclusion in a new German government. Two weeks later, after Himmler's abortive attempts to conclude a separate peace with the West had failed, he asked Wulf for astrological advice as to what he should do next. Wulf told him to escape to Sweden.

With the war all but over now, Himmler asked Wulf to predict the likelihood of air raids. Where in Germany would he be safest from bombing? Once again Wulf got out his charts and drew up astrological calculations. Soon, however, the strain of doing daily computations of such an insane nature became too much for him, and he left Himmler for good.

Perhaps the final word on the Nazis and astrology should be left to Himmler. He said,

> Astrology, as a universalist doctrine, is directly opposed to our own philosophical view of the world. A doctrine which is meant to apply in equal measure to Negroes, Indians, Chinese and Aryans is in opposition to our conception of the racial soul. Each one of the peoples I have named has its own specific racial soul.[15]

Between such a view of the world and the doctrine that an individual's sun sign was more important than the colour of his skin, there could indeed be no compromise. One can see in these words of Himmler not only why the Nazis did persecute the astrologers, but why, ideologically, they had to. For the Nazis viewed the occult in the same way that Stalin did science. Just as the Russian dictator spoke of 'capitalist physics' and 'proletarian physics', so, to the Nazis, there was 'Aryan astrology' and 'universalist astrology'. Between two such diametrically opposed views of the world, there could be no middle point; one or the other had to triumph. Large numbers of astrologers died in concentration camps under the Nazis. It may seem hard to see them as martyrs to the truth, but perhaps they were, in a deeper sense than they even suspected, martyrs to a higher truth.

4 | Racial Ramblings

We have already seen how the Nazis imported their racial mythology into the formerly 'universalist' system of astrology. However, Nazi racism was to take forms both more ludicrous and more sinister than its insistence on an Aryan astrology.

One of the founding fathers of German racism was Richard Wagner. The composer was deeply stirred by both German mythology and by the occult, and in his first opera, *Rienzi*, based on a novel by the English occultist Bulwer-Lytton, he clearly showed his occult preoccupations. This interest in mythology and the occult was to continue throughout his life. In a whole series of operas he took themes from German paganism and helped to foster the growing interest in the subject throughout the country.[1]

In spite, or perhaps because, of the fact that Wagner owed almost all his early success to Jewish acquaintances, he was violently anti-Semitic. He despised the Jews and wrote against them, seeing them as totally un-German. They were, he believed, a threat to the purity of both the German race and its culture. Wagner argued that only if foreign influences became Germanized would it be permissible for them to affect German culture. He described democracy as 'quite un-German', and as a 'disgusting transplanted Franco-Jewish-German perversion'.[2]

Many of Wagner's disciples took the composer's views to their logical conclusion and tried to revive the old German paganism. Wagner was not so consistent; instead, he tried to remake Christianity in his own image. According to him, Jesus was not a Jew, but an Aryan. He also displayed, especially in *Parsifal*, strong signs of Gnostic influences on his Christianity.

(The religion, whose gospels predate those of the New Testament, emphasizes knowledge, rather than faith, belief in the individual and contempt for worldly matters.) In Wagner's hands, Christianity suddenly teaches that salvation comes only through struggle, search and deep occult knowledge. Only the select few are capable of discovering its truth.

Wagner believed that it was his destiny to awaken the German people to their proud ancestry and their superiority to all other races. He claimed that in *Götterdämmerung* he was warning of 'the tragedy of modern capitalism and the spirit of Yiddish usury'.[3] But it was *Parsifal* which was to bring his obsessive racialism firmly into the public eye. Wagner and the philosopher Nietzsche had been friends and fellow admirers, but when Wagner told Nietzsche of his plans to compose the opera, Nietzsche felt disgusted at the idea of preaching Christian renunciation. He broke with Wagner and accused him of betraying German ideals.

Wagner retaliated by claiming that Jesus was an Aryan, that Nietzsche was Jewish – which he was not – and that he, Wagner, was busy trying to find 'a final solution' to 'the Jewish problem'. The phrase 'the Final Solution', which was to have such appalling consequences many years later, was first uttered by Wagner during his controversy with Nietzsche about Christianity.[4]

Wagner became a hero in occult circles. The French occultist Sar Peladan made a journey to Bayreuth and promptly claimed that Wagner 'possessed the soul of a natural magician'. In 1880 Wagner wrote a work called *Religion and Art*, in which he claimed that the function of art was to express divine truths. All truly inspired music, he said, had to be symbolic in conception. Wagner praised ecstatic religion, purity of soul, vegetarianism and the struggle for the spiritual regeneration of Germany. It seems odd to think that a man who advocated vegetarianism and anti-vivisection could also call for 'a final solution' to 'the Jewish problem'. However, Wagner was to find a pupil who managed to be equally firm in both beliefs: Adolf Hitler.[5]

Wagner had a decisive influence on his son-in-law, Houston Stewart Chamberlain. An Englishman who became a naturalized German, Chamberlain wrote a book which became notorious: *The Foundations of the Nineteenth Century*. He claimed that this work had been directed by the activities of devils. His principal obsession was, of course, the Aryan 'master race'. Chamberlain argued that there was no need for the 'racial degeneracy' brought about by intermarriage with 'inferior breeds'. Instead, a new 'higher race' could be systematically bred, in which the new supermen could dominate the world. Chamberlain was quite sure that it was the destiny of the German people to be the master race.[6]

If Wagner was simply a repulsive human being, Chamberlain was mentally disturbed. His constant struggles with devils which he believed were taking him over, his inability to write except in a state of nervous exaltation bordering on trance, are all clear signs of mental illness. He argued that 'the German mind must guide the Aryan peoples to racial supremacy and world domination'. He claimed that 'all civilization flows from the white race', and that every event in European history was the unaided accomplishment of the German race. He had to distort history enormously to maintain his theory, turning such men as Homer and Virgil into Germans.[7]

Predictably, Chamberlain was an extreme anti-Semite. He claimed that the Jewish race was seeking to 'infect the Indo-Europeans with Jewish blood'. The consequence would be, he claimed, that 'there would be in Europe only one single people of pure race, that of the Jews; all the rest would be a herd of pseudo-Hebraic mestizos, a people beyond all doubt degenerate physically, mentally, and morally'.[8] (It seems not to have occurred to Chamberlain that if all the Jews were intermixing with all the Aryans, not only the Aryans but also the Jews would also disappear as a people. But logic was never Chamberlain's strong point.)

His conception of an Aryan Christ was even more extreme than Wagner's. Chamberlain claimed that Jesus was a blond, blue-eyed Nordic, the son of a Galilean woman and a Roman soldier. But Chamberlain did not follow his father-in-law in wanting a German Christianity. Instead, he argued for a mysticism of blood and the soil. He called for a 'new God' to direct the spiritual regeneration of Germany. Kaiser Wilhelm invited him to court and told him, 'God sent your book to the German people.' The unhinged Chamberlain promptly decided that the Kaiser was the new God he had been looking for and placed his picture opposite Leonardo's study of the head of Christ. In his turn the Kaiser allowed Chamberlain to become a close confidant of the Imperial household. Before long he had become a kind of Rasputin, much to the alarm of German Intelligence.[9]

The extraordinary spectacle of an Englishman at the Imperial Court becoming the chief occult adviser to the Kaiser could be understood by the German espionage chiefs only if it was assumed that Chamberlain was a British spy. But nothing so rational was the case. The fact was that the mentally deranged British author and the German Emperor were equally obsessed with Nordic mysticism and German expansionism.

The German commander-in-chief, General von Moltke, was worried at the profound influence this English Rasputin was having on the Kaiser. Unlike the latter, von Moltke knew that Chamberlain wrote his works in a state of demonic possession. Von Moltke was also a disciple of Rudolf Steiner, who will also enter our story later. From Steiner he knew that Chamberlain dabbled with black magic and Satanism, that he was insane, and that his crazy ideas could well bring about the ruin of Germany.[10]

Not only did Chamberlain claim that Jesus was an Aryan; he also claimed that only Nordic races, especially the Germans, had the spiritual maturity to appreciate the real teachings of Christianity. Thus Christ shed his blood not for the world, but for the salvation of the Aryan race alone.

Through Wagner, Chamberlain became aware of the spiritual significance of the Spear of Destiny. The result was that he spent years studying the true significance of the spear and evolved – or invented – a whole chain of history for it over a period of 2,000 years. He saw the spear as a symbol of the magical powers residing in the blood of the race, and this started him off on his own racial theories.

In one of his demonic trances Chamberlain had a vision in which the Emperor Sigismund appeared to him. The Emperor told him that it was a sin to allow the spear to remain in the hands of the Austrians rather than the Germans. Chamberlain told the Kaiser of his vision and the Imperial historians discovered that Sigismund had indeed decreed that the spear should be permanently lodged in Germany. Since this came to light after a series of embarrassing foreign-policy reverses for Germany, the Kaiser decided that it was a matter of national security for the spear to be returned to the Fatherland. However, it was hardly likely that the Emperor of Austria would agree to give it back.

There followed an episode of pure farce. The Kaiser decided to arrange an exhibition of German art in Berlin, under cover of which he invited the senile Emperor of Austria to attend. He also invited him to lend to Germany, for the purposes of the exhibition, all the treasures and relics of the Holy Roman Empire. These, of course, included the Spear of Destiny.

Unfortunately for Kaiser Wilhelm, von Moltke got wind of the scheme. He wrote a secret note to the Austrian Emperor warning him that the Kaiser meant to keep the Spear when the exhibition had finished. This extraordinary event is surely the only time in history that a general has told a friendly monarch that his own ruler meant to steal an occult object from him. Hardly surprisingly, even the senile Emperor took exception to this. He sent the Kaiser a curt letter refusing to loan the treasures; neither the Kaiser nor Chamberlain ever did find out why.[11]

After the war Chamberlain became disillusioned with the Kaiser, turning his attention to a younger and more exciting leader. In 1923 he openly hailed Hitler as the future saviour of Germany. The latter responded by calling Chamberlain 'the Father of National Socialism'.[12]

Another important influence on German racist mythology was Adolf Lanz. Lanz had delusions of grandeur and claimed that his father was Baron Lancz von Liebenfels, and took to styling himself thus.

Lanz published a magazine called *Ostara* which combined the zanier fringes of occultism with the worst racialist excesses: he regarded Czechs, Slovenes and Jews as being subhuman. He laid down strict criteria for membership of an occult order called the New Templars, which he founded. As well as the usual prerequisite of blond hair and blue eyes, members also had to have tiny hands and feet and large heads. This mishmash of racial fantasy he called 'ariosophy'. Among other things ariosophy involved the scriptural interpretation that angels were Aryan heroes. He believed that all the subhuman races dated back to Atlantis and Lemuria. Mankind had not evolved from apes; apes had degenerated from men. Jews and other inferior races had arisen through the intermixing of blood between apes and humans. This occult-racial gibberish had an even more sinister side, however: Lanz thought of the Aryans as the master race; the rest of humanity was fit only for slavery or extermination. Among his other unattractive features, Lanz was the first person definitely known to have advocated the Final Solution. Not content with maintaining the purity of the Aryans by selective breeding, he also advocated the extermination of 'inferior' races. For those who engaged in 'inter-racial sexual relationships', he urged forced labour and a starvation diet as punishments. One can see in these ravings the roots of the concentration camps and the Nuremberg laws forbidding sexual contact between Aryans and Jews.

That these prejudices were common to Hitler and Lanz was not accidental: Hitler admired Lanz, read his magazine regularly and even met him on a number of occasions. He gave Hitler personal occult teaching, and in 1932 boasted, 'Hitler is one of our pupils.' In 1934 Lanz proudly claimed that his order was the first manifestation of Nazism.[13]

Another writer who had a profound influence on the racist elements in German occultism was actually a Frenchman called Saint-Yves d'Alveydre. He pretended to be a French marquis and was indeed so mad that even his own father said of him, 'Of all the lunatics I have known my son is the most dangerous.' Saint-Yves was not, except in one particular, even an original thinker. He simply stole most of his ideas, sometimes word for word, from another French racist occult writer called Fabre d'Olivet. The only original element Saint-Yves added was 'the underground city of Agartha'. This, he claimed, was a city in Tibet, of whose existence he had been made aware by telepathic communication from the Dalai Lama. He also claimed that 'a high official of the Hindu Church' – whatever that was[14] – had told him about the city of Agartha. This high official turned out to be a pet-shop owner in Le Havre. Saint-Yves also stole ideas from another eccentric French political philosopher called Fourier, who believed, among other things, that technological progress would lead to a socialist society in which all animals would become vegetarian and the sea would turn into lemonade. But it was the story of Agartha which attracted the Nazis to

Saint-Yves's writings. In due course it was to have a profound effect upon them, as we shall see presently.[15]

Another theory which soon became inextricably entwined with German racist politics was the doctrine of geopolitics. This was invented by a British imperialist called Sir Halford Mackinder at the turn of the century to justify colonial expansion. It was soon being expressed by German reactionaries, in an even cruder form than Mackinder's, as the concept of *Lebensraum* or 'living-space'. All great nations were supposed to have this need and in its pursuit they engaged in war, to expand the amount of territory under their control. The leading German 'expert' in geopolitics was Karl Haushofer, a professor of geopolitics at Munich University.[16]

In addition to his ideas on geopolitics, Haushofer also subscribed to the equally unscientific theory of historionomy. This was the idea – not, admittedly, a new one – that all history was racial history. He believed that the Aryan race had originated in central Asia and that the Germans therefore had a right to reclaim that territory for their own. The eastern boundary of this Aryan empire, which existed only in Haushofer's vivid imagination, was Tibet. The vast tracts of territory to which Haushofer was referring he called, adopting a phrase of Mackinder's, the 'heartland'. Both Mackinder and Haushofer believed that whoever controlled the heartland automatically achieved world domination. He went on to claim that all civilization was exclusively Aryan and that the root of Aryan civilization was the heartland.[17]

But the racial mythology to which Hitler subscribed was far more extreme than the simple prejudice of the average German anti-Semite. It was the peculiar racial interpretation of history which Hitler learned from an organization which we shall describe in the following chapter, the Thule group.

According to Thulist racial mythology, the first men had no physical bodies and were sexless. Their creators were called Chohans and came from the moon. A second race, which evolved bodies, was also developed by the Chohans. They did not die, and eventually the first race became absorbed into the second. The third race was hermaphrodite, but later it divided into male and female. The apes resulted from a cross-breeding between these people and female animals: apes are therefore fallen men. The fourth race had consciousness and speech, and a complete division of the sexes. Thule was the first kingdom. The next kingdom was Lemuria, whose sole remnant is Tiahuanaco, an ancient ruined city high in the South American mountains – a testimony of its existence.

Only one group of representatives of the Lemurian elite still survives, the men of Shamballah, a secret oasis in the Gobi Desert. We shall have more to say of them later too. A degenerate branch of the Lemurians became hunters and cavemen, whose last visible living representatives are the Australian aborigines. The next race was Atlantis; and, of course, the Nordic race is Atlantean. Hitler and the Thulists believed that they were the descendants of the secret chiefs, and therefore the master race.[18]

Further ammunition for the occult-racial mythology in Germany was provided by Alfred Rosenberg, who was part Estonian, French and Jewish. The Bolshevik Revolution filled Rosenberg with hatred. He said that ninety per cent of the Russian Communists he met were Jewish. In spite of his Jewish ancestry Rosenberg was convinced that he was pure German, even though after six years of living in Germany he was still incapable of writing the language grammatically.

Rosenberg met another important figure whom we shall meet in the next chapter, Dietrich Eckart. He took Rosenberg under his wing after reading the Estonian Jew's manuscript, *The Russian Jewish Revolution*. Soon Rosenberg had completed another work, *The Trace of the Jew through Changing Times*, in which he accused the Jews of being responsible for socialism, anarchism and capitalism. They were also apparently behind the Freemasons, and, as England was both the headquarters of Freemasonry and 'the centre of world Jewry', England was the natural enemy of the Aryan race.[19]

In 1919 Rosenberg met Hitler at Eckart's home. The two men were greatly taken by one another and Rosenberg added a pseudoscientific veneer to the occult anti-Semitism both men shared. Rosenberg also persuaded the Nazis to add the Freemasons to the list of enemies of Germany. He soon became the party's official 'ideologist', with the job of providing 'facts' to back up the campaign against the Jews.[20]

Rosenberg was also responsible for two works which were to

bring death and destruction to millions and provide a 'warrant for genocide'. The first of these was the notorious *Protocols of the Learned Elders of Zion*. Rosenberg did not write this, but he prepared the first German edition for the press and added an extensive commentary. The *Protocols* were supposed to be an account of the secret proceedings of 'World Jewry' for the purpose of establishing world domination.

There was even an occult touch to the way in which Rosenberg came into possession of the *Protocols*. As he sat in his study, a man whom he had never seen before and never saw again, entered the room without knocking. Placing the book on his desk, the stranger vanished into thin air without a word![21] So at least Rosenberg claimed. In fact, as he knew perfectly well, the manuscript was a forgery. But he also knew that in the right hands, it could provide a stepping-stone to power. By showing the *Protocols* to Eckart, in spite of his Jewish ancestry, Rosenberg was admitted to the Thule group and the Nazi Party. The work itself became an astonishing bestseller, being translated and published all over the world. Even British papers seriously considered whether or not action should be taken against the Jews in the light of the *Protocols*.[22]

The *Protocols* had been forged by a Russian occultist called Nilus. He had taken care to incorporate them into a remarkably prophetic document by the Russian philosopher Soloviev, *The Anti-Christ*, in which he predicted that the Antichrist would come into the world in human form. He would persecute the Jews in particular. Soloviev even prophesied that the skins of Jews would be turned into household ornaments – thus anticipating the dreadful uses to which the Nazis later put them, such as for lampshades. But even more remarkably Soloviev foretold the year in which the Antichrist would come to power: 1921. That year Hitler became leader of the Nazi Party. He also predicted that the Antichrist would be thirty-three years old when he assumed a position of power; and again this matched the Führer's age.[23]

As well as introducing the *Protocols* into Germany, Rosenberg also wrote a bizarre work of his own, *The Myth of the Twentieth Century*. This came to be second only to *Mein Kampf* as a Nazi bible. Rosenberg believed that everything was part of God, and that the soul became one with God at 'the ground of a man's being'.

Races [he added] are God's thoughts. Race is the external form of soul. From this secret core there develops what we call racial characteristic and race culture. For Aryan man the true religious experience has always been outside space and time and non-causal, that is, non-materialistic, non-historical and non-rational.

The true religion for a German was a 'religion of the blood'. Christianity, being Jewish, was unsuitable.[24]

Hitler, of course, was to go beyond even Rosenberg's anti-Semitism. On one occasion he told the German governor of Danzig, Rauschning, that the Jews were not only subhuman, they were literally children of the Devil! 'The Jew,' said Hitler, 'is the anti-man, the creature of another God. He must have come from another root of the human race. Not that I would call the Jew a beast. He is much further from the beasts than we Aryans. He is a creature outside nature and alien to nature.'[25]

There is some evidence that Hitler actually believed the Jews to be the last living representatives of the prehistoric Neanderthal man. He was also contemptuous of Christianity. 'Whether it is the Old Testament or the New it's all the same old Jewish swindle. One is either a German or a Christian. You cannot be both. We need free men who feel and know that God is in themselves.' He also called conscience 'a Jewish invention, a blemish like circumcision'. 'Through the peasantry,' Hitler claimed, 'we shall really be able to destroy Christianity, because there is in them a true religion rooted in nature and blood.'[26]

There can be no doubt from these and similar passages that Rosenberg's influence on Hitler was decisive. In fact it was so obvious that the Estonian refugee had influenced Hitler that when the Nazi leader became Chancellor of Germany he immediately suppressed a book by Eckart which made the extent of this indebtedness evident.

The Thule Group

5

Thule was supposed to have been an island somewhere in the frozen wastes of the far north. It had belonged to a once immense northern continent before disappearing from off the face of the earth. There was considerable disagreement among the occultists as to the precise whereabouts of the island.

But the myth of Thule went far beyond the question of whether or not such an island or continent existed. Before long it had become associated with the myth of some remote golden age in which blond, blue-eyed, vegetarian Nordics presided over the earliest human civilizations.

The Thule group was founded around 1918 – possibly earlier, certainly no later – by two men: Baron von Sebottendorf and Walter Nauhaus. Von Sebottendorf was a member of many occult orders, and in no way entitled to his aristocratic title. In fact, he was the son of an engine-driver. But inventing titles was a pastime which seemed to flourish among the lunatic fringe of the political right. Nauhaus was a former soldier who had been invalided out of the army. Between them they set out to make the Thule group a powerful force in Bavarian politics.[1]

The two driving forces in the Thule Group, however, were Eckart and Haushofer. We have already touched briefly on both men, but now we shall study their occult career in more detail. Eckart was a visionary who was both an alcoholic and a drug addict. He was also completely mad. The two groups of people he hated more than any others were women and Jews. He regarded women as fit for child-bearing and nothing else. As for the Jews, Eckart blamed them for his lack of success as a writer and decided that his failure was the result of a deliberate Jewish conspiracy to suppress his work. He decided to write and publish an anti-Semitic news-sheet, 'Auf gut Deutsch' – 'In good German'. In this newspaper he gave full vent to his various occult-racial obsessions.

Eckart said that the world was evil. All existence is in the material world, which is an illusion. But the supremacy of matter needs to be overcome; and the only way to do this is through death. According to Eckart, Jesus believed this. However, his message had been corrupted by St Paul and other Christians. The arch-enemies of true Christianity were, of course, the Jews. Only the Germans had sufficient spirituality to appreciate the true religion.[2]

Eckart spent much of his life in a lunatic asylum, where he managed to stage some of his plays that no one else would touch. These incorporated neo-pagan rituals, scenes from German mythology and the grail stories. One of Eckart's plays which he and his fellow inmates performed in the asylum was about the Spear of Destiny itself.[3]

Eckart's principal obsessions were anti-Semitism, his Aryan Christianity and the history of Islam. He believed himself to be the reincarnation of a ninth-century black magician from Muslim Spain. Eckart joined the Thule group and turned it from being a bunch of cranks who believed that all Germans were the last living representatives of Atlantis into a sinister order practising Satanism and black magic.[4]

Hitler himself was a member of the Thule group and soon became a close friend of Eckart. It was the crazed Eckart who initiated Hitler into appalling rituals involving rape, sadism and even human sacrifice. This was the last thing Eckart did before he finally died after years of alcoholic poisoning and drug abuse.[5]

Just before his own death, Eckart said, 'Follow Hitler. He will dance but it is I who called the tune. We have given him the means of communication with Them. Do not mourn for me; I shall have influenced history more than any other German.' By 'them', Eckart meant the Secret Chiefs, the magical masters from the spirit world.[6]

Eckart conveyed to Hitler the secrets of black magic on several different levels. He not only taught him how to contact the Secret Chiefs, but also how to be attuned to psychic revelations. Hitler learned from Eckart the means of psychically harnessing the physical world, the control and focusing of willpower, and one of the key magical techniques, visualization.[7]

Like Hitler, Eckart was obsessed with the Spear of Destiny and the grail legends. Eckart went to Sicily and discovered the now ruined temple of Erix, where, in the old days, the priestesses of Venus had held their rites to the goddess of love. Hitler believed himself to be a reincarnation of Landulf of Capua, whom he identified as the historical original of the black magician Klingsor in the grail legends. Eckart discovered that Landulf fled to this old sanctuary when his betrayal of Christianity had been discovered. There, he conducted horrible black magic rituals, involving human sacrifice. As we have seen already, Eckart repeated this series of Satanic rituals with Hitler just before his own death, to initiate the future dictator into his final pact with the powers of darkness.[8]

What Eckart achieved as a result of these disgusting perversions was to open up the *chakras* (or centres of vital energy) in Hitler's subtle or astral body. As a result of these rituals Hitler was able to communicate directly with the powers of darkness. Even in death, Eckart's legacy of hate pursued the servants of light. His last dying wishes were that the Goetheanum, the headquarters of Steiner's Anthroposophical movement, should be burned to the ground, along with its founder. Eckart, one of the most dangerous black magicians of the twentieth century, was bitterly hostile to the outstanding white magician, Steiner.[9]

On Eckart's instructions, this actually happened. Steiner was lecturing to a large crowd when the building burst into flames. Steiner and his audience managed to escape only because the Nazi who set the fire allowed too much time for it to catch. Two years later Steiner rebuilt the building, just before his death – of natural causes.

Although the Thule group included many rich and powerful men, not one of them had an ounce of charisma. The Thulists were keenly aware of this lack and Eckart in particular, who was waiting for the arrival of a German messiah, was acutely pained by it. And we must not forget the kind of messiah that Eckart was waiting for. Every one of the inner circle of the Thule group were black magicians and Satanists. In their monstrous rituals the darkest deeds known to occultism were habitually carried out. Sexual perversion and human sacrifice were their stock-in-trade. They also engaged in political assassination. When the Munich chief of police, himself a member of the Thulists, was asked by a member of the Bavarian government if he knew about the existence of murder gangs in Bavaria, he gave the notorious reply, 'Yes, but not enough of them.'[10]

Within the four years between 1919 and 1923, over 300 political assassinations were carried out. In addition an astonishingly high number of people, especially in Munich, disappeared in mysterious circumstances. Most of them were simply murdered as human sacrifices in acts of black magic carried out by the Thule group and with the full knowledge and co-operation of the local police.[11]

The other key member of the Thulists, besides Eckart, was Haushofer. He was a friend of Eckart's and also belonged to another highly influential occult order, the Vril Society. One of his pupils was Hess, who later claimed that Haushofer was one of the Secret Chiefs. Whether or not this is true, there is no doubt that his influence on Hitler was decisive.

As well as his theories of geopolitics and historionomy, which we have already come across, Haushofer was an even more accomplished black magician than Eckart. Where the drug-ridden and alcoholic Eckart could only operate on one level, Haushofer was a man of extraordinary talents.

It is not too much to say that Haushofer was the evil genius who completed the Satanic transformation of Hitler into a being of almost supernatural dimensions. In comparison with men like Pretzsche, even Eckart, Haushofer was a master magician.

The entire inner circle of the Thule Group were all practitioners of the black arts. But none ever achieved the potency of Haushofer. This cold, calculating, almost academic occultist gave Hitler a deadly purpose which the more mercurial Eckart could never have furnished him with.

During the chaos that followed the overthrow of imperial Germany, the Thulists were one of the few groups with a coherent plan and programme. Their biggest handicap was, and remained for some time, the lack of a credible leader. In face of this crisis, the Thulist inner circle sat down and debated the entire situation. What was needed, they decided, was not anyone who had been associated with imperial Germany. As Eckart himself put it, 'We need a man at the head who can stand the sound of a machine gun. We can't use an officer because people don't respect them any more. The best man for the job would be a worker who knows how to talk.'[12]

Two Thulists founded the German Workers Party in response to this crisis. Before long, as we know, Hitler was to join it and turn it into the Nazi Party. When he became the leader two years later, he soon found himself engaged in a bitter struggle for control with the Thulists. They felt that, as the men who had made Hitler, he ought to be answerable to them.

It was not long before Hitler and the Thulists were openly quarrelling. In spite of his indebtedness to the Thulists, he was totally contemptuous of them as any sort of political force. As he remarked in *Mein Kampf*:

> If anything is contrary to the spirit of the people it is juggling with ancient Germanic expressions. I warn again and again against these wandering *völkisch* scholars whose positive achievement is always nothing, but whose conceit cannot be matched. The same persons who wave about toy swords, carefully manufactured in imitation of old Germanic style, and wear a prepared bearskin with bull's horns to cover their bearded heads, always preach for the present time only a spiritual battle and quickly run away from the sight of a communist blackjack. I got to know these people too well not to feel digust at this miserable comedy. Despite all proofs of their total inability these people pretend to understand everything better than anybody else. Especially in regard to the so-called religious reformers of the ancient German type, I have the feeling that they are sent by dark forces who do not desire the rebirth of our people. For their entire activity leads the *Volk* away from its fight against the common enemy, the Jew, in order that it may expend its energy in internal religious struggles.[13]

This passage is not entirely truthful, but it certainly illustrates Hitler's contempt for those occultists who were content to keep to the paths of ritual rather than mix it in with the hurly-burly of politics. It has to be remembered, too, that when Hitler wrote these words he was fighting a battle for control of the Nazi Party against the occult wing of the movement. But the curious thing is that, throughout the writing of *Mein Kampf*, Hitler was in constant touch with a Catholic priest who belonged to the Thule group, as well as with Haushofer. Though Hitler certainly never abandoned his own occult-racial views he did stop trusting the occultists. This was one of the main reasons that they were the first people to be persecuted when the Nazis finally came to power.[14]

Hitler not only believed in occult powers: he actually made use of them over the years to help himself to supremacy. The important thing for him was that there should be no dangerous competition from other occultists. To this end he set out to establish a monopoly of occult and magical power for the Nazi Party. So obsessed were the Nazis with the idea of making all thinking in Germany conform to their own views that on one occasion it manifested itself in unintentionally ludicrous form. In 1938, a Nazi banner was suspended over the front of Wittenau Lunatic Asylum. The message read, 'This establishment supports the Führer unconditionally.' When Nazis could regard it as worthwhile to advertise that lunatics supported them their paranoia had clearly reached truly manic proportions.[15]

6 | One Foot in Atlantis

Hermann Rauschning, governor of Danzig, and a man at one time very close to Hitler, recorded many of their conversations together in his book *Hitler Speaks*. Rauschning is quite explicit about Hitler's occult obsessions.

'At bottom,' Rauschning said, 'every German has one foot in Atlantis, where he seeks a better Fatherland and a better patrimony. This double nature of the Germans, this faculty they have of splitting their personality, which enables them to live in the real world and at the same time to project themselves into an imaginary world, is especially noticeable in Hitler and provides the key to his magic socialism.' He added sarcastically, 'National Socialism is the St Vitus' dance of the twentieth century.'[1]

Atlantis has been located in numerous places, even in outer space; but the most popular theories have always been those that place it in the Atlantic Ocean, in Britain, or somewhere in the northern regions. Nowadays historians regard the whole Atlantis story as a confused memory of Minoan Crete. However, this theory has never been romantic enough to attract the Atlantologists. In Germany and Denmark there was particular determination to 'prove' that Atlantis was really in Denmark, or Germany, or any other northern land which could be claimed as a remote relation.

Himmler was particularly keen on the views of a certain Hermann Wirth regarding Atlantis. When, in 1935, Himmler set up the Ahnenerbe, the Nazi Occult Bureau, Wirth was appointed its first head. It soon distinguished itself by a combination of lunatic views and a total inability to produce any practical results.[2]

Wirth believed that Atlantis was situated at the North Pole and that all civilization stemmed from the mysterious region. Naturally, the Atlanteans were blond, blue-eyed Nordics.[3] Wirth was particularly impressed by the *Oera Linda* book, a nineteenth-century forgery which 'proved' that all true civilization had been founded by the Germans.[4] Now, at Danzig and also at Königsberg Universities there was a professor who was unwise enough to publicly ridicule the *Oera Linda*. The result was that Wirth appealed to Himmler to prevent the professor from continuing to criticize the book. Himmler agreed with Wirth and proceeded to 'put the fear of God' into both the offending individual and German academics generally. Wirth was given full powers by Himmler to set up an occult equivalent to the traditional academic and scientific institutions.[5]

Under Wirth's leadership, the Occult Bureau tried hard to 'research' prehistoric times in an attempt to determine the truth of the *Oera Linda* book and Atlantis generally. One of his favourite theories was that put forward by Olof Rudbeck in 1675, which claimed that Atlantis had been in Sweden.[6] Naturally he claimed that all civilization flowed from this Swedish source.

Rudbeck's theory was taken up by various German occultists after the First World War and combined with Madame Blavatsky's Theosophical Society account of world 'history', as well as the inevitable Aryan racial doctrines. Before long the definitive version of this lunatic rag-bag had been put forward by K.G. Zschaetch in a book published in 1922 called *Atlantis: The Original Home of the Aryans*. This again placed Atlantis at the North Pole, populated by blond-haired, blue-eyed Aryans. Using a process called 'racial memory' Zschaetch announced that Atlantis had been destroyed as the result of the Earth colliding with a comet. Only three survivors of the deluge escaped: these were Wotan, who became a god, his pregnant sister and his daughter. All three were vegetarians and teetotallers. On escaping from Atlantis, this Nordic family took shelter from the deluge in the roots of an enormous cabbage, greater in height than any tree, and placed on the brink of a convenient cold spring. (Zschaetch obviously considered this environment to be paradise.) However, Wotan's sister died in childbirth, sheltering among the cabbage roots. Thankfully, her child was fed by a convenient she-wolf, and from this event originated the story of Romulus and Remus.

Unfortunately for Wotan, his nephew did not marry his cousin. Instead of choosing a pure Nordic vegetarian teetotaller for his bride, he chose instead to fornicate with 'lesser' racial breeds. They taught him to eat meat and consume alcohol. Alcoholic drink was invented by a Jewish woman called Heid, who had learned how to ferment the fruit of the cabbage plant. In those ways the Jews introduced the corruptions of racial impurity, drunkenness and meat-eating into the formerly pure Aryan race.[7]

According to Zschaetch, the majority of the myths and legends of the world are simply distorted racial recollections of these original events in Atlantis. The she-wolf suckling Wotan's grandson turned into Romulus and Remus; Heid's invention of alcohol became Eve offering Adam the apple: and the cabbage became Yggdrasil, the world-tree of Norse mythology.

Taking ideas from Zschaetch and the *Oera Linda* book, among other sources, Wirth managed to convince Himmler of the truth of his speculations. He believed that by continual contemplation of the symbols and legends of ancient peoples, he had been able to discover their true significance. This 'intuitive' approach to scholarship he apparently shared with his wife. Above the door of his home there hung a notice which read, 'No Smoking, A Deep Breather Lives Here.' The deep breather was his wife. Apparently she was so absorbed in her deep breathing that she hardly ever spoke. Instead she sat, staring broodily into space, trying to make contact with whatever powers from the spirit world she could meet. Through telepathy she transmitted their thoughts to her husband, who in his turn translated them into words. Or so at least Wirth and his wife claimed.[8]

Wirth's 'intuitive' decipherment of ancient symbolism, together with his wife's communications from the spirit world, led him to declare with complete confidence that Atlantis and Thule were one and the same continent. The lost land, however, did not lie in the submerged waters of the Atlantic Ocean, but in the region of the Arctic. This continent had once been an advanced civilization, worshipping one God and engaged in many expeditions to other parts of the world. Even the Nordic race was not pure; they were the result of marriage between the Thulean/Atlanteans with 'lesser' breeds. The last surviving examples of the original race were the Sadlermiut Eskimos, who, alas, were a degenerate specimen of the breed. They are now, of course, extinct.[9]

Rosenberg also believed that Atlantis lay in the frozen north. He explained away the various religious symbols, and in particular the swastika, as being based upon earlier racial memories of an Arctic sun. Oswald Spengler, whose *The Decline of the West* was to have a profound influence upon Nazism, also adopted the belief in a northern Atlantis. Even the anti-Nazi Steiner gave serious attention to the hypothesis in his various writings on the legendary region. But it was Zschaetch and Wirth's myth of a race of blond-haired, blue-eyed Nordic Atlanteans living in Asgard (the home of the Gods in Norse and Teutonic mythology) which captured the imagination of the occult-minded among the Nazi Party.[10]

Steiner claimed that Atlantis was founded by refugees from Lemuria, another mythical continent, this time supposed to lie somewhere beneath the Pacific Ocean. The practice of black magic, according to Steiner, was responsible for the destruction of Atlantis. The inhabitants were said to be gifted with exceptional power, such as the ability to hear grass grow and see through the bark of trees. Their nights were spent in astral travelling, communing with the gods. Steiner claimed that the kings of Atlantis were guided by spirits from the gods, who ruled men through their leaders. Then matter was born, then intelligence, and the gods departed from among men. Left to themselves, without their spirit-guides, men turned to black magic, and Atlantis shared the fate which had formerly befallen Lemuria. However, a few Atlanteans escaped and their descendants founded the civilizations of Europe, Asia and Africa. Among his other ideas, Steiner was convinced that the Atlanteans possessed airships. After the dispersal of the natives of Atlantis, the Gobi Desert was drained and a number of black magicians escaped into Tibet. Of this Tibetan connection we shall have more to say later.[11]

Many Nazis and their sympathizers seized upon the idea that the Atlanteans were the 'sons of God' spoken of in Genesis, and that their intermarriage with 'the daughters of men' had led to the degeneration of the race. This association of Atlantis with

Nordic racial mythology was a constant preoccupation among occultists of the early twentieth century.[12]

The general line taken by German occultists on Atlantis was, first, to locate it in the northern regions, preferably at the Arctic Circle. From the Arctic, the Nordic/Atlantean race came into Europe, and spread German culture throughout the world. Admittedly, such men as Zschaetch made even more extravagant claims; but what else could be expected of a man who considered himself the last living descendant of the Greek god Zeus, of which his own name was a corruption?[13]

Mention has already been made of the *Oera Linda* book as a work which deeply interested both Wirth and Himmler. This added yet another 'lost land' to the occult mythology: Atland. This land was contemporary with but survived Atlantis, and lay between Greenland and the Hebrides. Some unexplained catastrophe destroyed the country and the survivors, known as Frisians, sailed the world, founding colonies – Minerva, Vesta, Woden, Neptune and Minos – as they went. Thus all civilization stems from these Frisian culture-heroes, whom later generations deified. They were even said to have founded the Inca Empire.[14]

As we have seen, when a German professor dared to publicly criticize the *Oera Linda* book as unhistorical, he received a rebuke from Himmler which terrified him into silence. To the Nazi occultists, Atlantis held a special place in their heart. It was their myth of a Golden Age, a lost paradise where Nordic supermen ruled the world. And it was just such a state of magical world-rulers that the Nazis looked to revive by force of arms in the twentieth century. Considering that the earliest accounts of Atlantis state that it was the wickedness of the place which led to its eventual downfall, and considering the deliberate practice of black magic and Satanism by many leading Nazis, the parallels between Germany and Atlantis are not accidental. Even to those Nazis who did not believe in Atlantis, it was in a very real sense the myth by which and for which they lived and died.[15] The extent to which the Atlantis myth dominated Nazi thinking can be gauged by the fact that the Germans actually thought it worth while to send out an expedition to the Baltic Sea in the hope of discovering the region's relics. That a modern technologically advanced state like Germany could consider it worthwhile to pour government funding into such a project, shows how deeply occultism had entered into the counsels of the men who ran Germany. So powerful a magnet for them was the faint chance of finding a northern Atlantis that they preferred to allocate money and resources to that outside possibility rather than spend it on work which might have actually changed the course of the war, such as the atomic bomb.[16]

Before long, virtually all German thinking on Atlantis had become inextricably mixed up with another theory, the glacial cosmogony of Hans Hoerbiger. To this new and even more bizarre aspect of Nazi occultism we shall now turn our attention.

7 Fire and Frost

The *Welteislehre*, or 'world ice theory', also known as 'glacial cosmogony', was a major preoccupation of both Himmler and Hitler. The theory was first put forward by an Austrian engineer called Hoerbiger. He believed in a highly complicated cosmology in which, to begin with, the moon was made of ice. From this idea it followed that the origin of the solar system must have been produced by blocks of ice colliding with the sun. Hoerbiger explained the absence of any facts to support his theory by means of something he called 'gravitational shadow'. When asked what this was, Hoerbiger simply used to shout at his critics: 'When will you learn that mathematics is valueless?'[1]

The present moon, Hoerbiger believed, was only the latest in a long series of previous earthly satellites. All planets spiral towards the sun, into which they will eventually fall and be consumed. As the planets approach the sun more closely, they are captured by the earth's gravitational field and become satellites. Now the force of gravity pulls them downwards, towards the earth. Eventually they are pulled into the earth's atmospheric field and break up, the debris of this disintegration falling upon the earth. This then becomes moonless again till the eventual capture of another satellite. All such events are accompanied by fire and flood. There have been at least six previous moons before our present moon was captured. Each capture and each subsequent collapse on the earth was responsible for such events as the biblical flood. The Book of Revelation is a mythological rendering of racial memories of the capture-collapse model.[2]

According to Hoerbiger and his followers, the present moon

69

was captured 15,000 years ago. The various folk memories of this catastrophe have come in the form of myths and legends. What they claimed is that as the moon approaches the earth, its gravitational pull increases. This increased the tides until they turn into a 'girdle-tide', a massive section of water centred around the equator. 250,000 years ago this effect led to the centre of world civilization being at Tiahuanaco.[3]

Tiahuanaco is a city in the Andes, situated at the forbidding altitude of 13,000 feet, with very remarkable ruins. It contains some striking megalithic constructions about whose age there is considerable dispute. To the question as to why they were built at so great a height, no orthodox historian has yet provided a convincing explanation. The followers of Hoerbiger claim that Tiahuanaco was once at ground level and only the collapse of the moon on the earth, with the consequent receding of the girdle-tide, left the city of Tiahuanaco stranded. There is, of course, no evidence at all for this assumption; but neither is there for any of the orthodox explanations. And the Tiahuanaco ruins are a genuinely striking and baffling problem for archaeologists.[4]

After the end of the First World War, a Germany in defeat and economic depression turned eagerly to every kind of crank and charlatan. Hoerbiger and his followers launched a whole series of books and articles advocating the world ice theory. At ordinary astronomical meetings they would interrupt other astronomers with cries of 'Out with orthodoxy, we want Hoerbiger.' Hoerbiger informed his opponents that they had a choice between believing in him or being treated as an enemy. In many ways his approach was a mirror-image of Hitler's to politics.[5]

During the 1920s the world ice theory began to win support in the German-speaking countries, appealing to the wave of irrationalism sweeping over Germany and Austria. To those who considered such things important, it also provided a pseudo-scientific rationale for the sinking of Atlantis beneath the ocean. As we saw in the last chapter, there were a lot of Atlantologists in Germany at this time. To them, Hoerbiger's theory seemed a confirmation of what they had always believed. For many of the occultists this was a decisive point in favour of the theory.[6]

Hoerbiger explained the sinkings of Atlantis, Lemuria and Mu and all the other legendary sunken lands by the capture of moons by the earth and their subsequent collapse upon it. The increased pull of gravity and gravitational shadow was also held to explain the folk tales of giants walking the face of the Earth. Even the appearance and disappearance of the dinosaurs were attributed to the same mechanisms. They also explained the biblical story of the sun standing still for Joshua.[7]

Although Hoerbiger died in 1931, his ideas became popular among *völkisch* occultists. They were particularly attractive to many members of the Nazi Party. In fact, most Hoerbigerians welcomed Hitler's appointment as Chancellor. They hoped that this would give them the ability to replace the 'traditional' physics and astronomy with Hoerbigerian cosmology. They issued a manifesto on Hitler's accession to power, claiming that, 'Our Nordic ancestors grew strong in ice and snow; belief in World Ice is consequently the natural heritage of Nordic Man.'[8]

To a great extent, the Hoerbigerians did at least succeed in having their cosmology taken seriously. Both Hitler and Himmler were particularly keen on the world ice theory. Hitler first came upon Hoerbiger's theories just before the First World War, during the time he was eagerly visiting the occult booksellers in the dingy backstreets of Vienna. There was also a Hungarian Catholic bishop, Ottocar Prohaszka, who was responsible for a Hungarian fascist group, and who was not only a personal friend of Hoerbiger but also close to several of the top Nazis between 1924 and 1927.[9] Himmler seems to have discovered the world ice theory through this anti-Semitic bishop. There was no doubt that the future head of the SS was deeply impressed by the theory. When he became a member of the Nazi government, Himmler set up the Nazi Occult Bureau, the editor of whose official magazine was a dedicated Hoerbigerian. He was also a close friend of another believer in the ever more influential mishmash of Atlantean and Horbigerian theory, a man named Kiss.[10]

Kiss was sufficiently persuasive to get Himmler to subsidize an expedition to Ethiopia in 1936 for the purpose of discovering pieces of former moons which had fallen on earth. Himmler also set up a meteorological department of the Occult Bureau which tried to produce weather forecasts on the basis of the world ice theory. Himmler further distinguished himself by actually announcing that, as the head of the SS, he was 'taking the world ice theory under his protection'.[11]

Himmler used to deluge Nazi Party members with works of Hoerbigerian cosmology, at the same time getting the Gestapo to suppress any criticism of it. At one point he even insisted that the German expedition to the Himalayas should spend its time carrying out Hoerbigerian experiments.[12]

So keen was Himmler to encourage Hoerbiger's theory that many Nazis got the impression that to progress in the Party you had to believe in the world ice theory. Other Nazi occultists in high places, jealous of their own rival theories, took alarm at this. Certainly the world ice theory was rapidly advancing to the status of a semi-official cosmology.

Rosenberg decided to strike back at the Hoerbigerians, whose views he did not share. In a circular which he issued in 1937, and sent to all party officers, Rosenberg made his own position clear. 'The Party can in no circumstances take towards these questions an attitude of ideological dogmatism.' Nor did Goering subscribe to the world ice theory, preferring instead an even more bizarre cosmology, which we shall examine in the next chapter. But Goebbels, Himmler and Hitler were all convinced and ardent supporters of Hoerbiger's theory.[13]

In so far as Nazi Germany ever had any occult cosmology which attained more or less general acceptance among party members, it was Hoerbigerian cosmology. Although to this day there remain disciples of the world ice theory, never again has it gained the power over the minds of men that it did during the years of Nazi domination. It was vaunted as 'a genuinely Aryan intellectual treasure'. As we shall discover later, this particular 'asset' played a key role in losing the Germans the war on the Russian Front.

Hitler himself said,

> I'm quite inclined to accept the cosmic theories of Hoerbiger. It's not impossible that there was a clash between the Earth and the Moon that gave the Moon its present orbit. It's also possible that the Earth attracted to itself the atmosphere of the Moon and that this radically altered the conditions of life on our planet. It was a great step forward in the days of Ptolemy to say that the Earth was a sphere and that the stars circulated around it.

Copernicus in his turn has been largely left behind. In our time Hoerbiger has made another step forward. The real question is whether the Earth came from the Sun or whether it has a tendency to approach it.[14]

Hitler and Hoerbiger actually met several times before the cosmologist died in 1931. At these meetings he ranted and raved at Hitler in the fashion the Nazi leader used on his entourage. When Hitler tried to assert himself, Hoerbiger simply, and repeatedly, told him to shut up. Even Hitler was unable to outface Hoerbiger's colossal self-conceit. The idea of the future master of most of Europe being shouted down by this cranky cosmologist is almost incredible; yet it actually happened.[15]

It was not long before Hoerbiger's ideas were being combined by keen Nazis with Rosenberg's Nordic mythology. One such pamphlet was published in 1936, and claimed that the relation between Einstein's theory of relativity to Hoerbiger's world ice theory was 'as the Talmud is to the Edda'.[16]

Before long, however, as the theory became increasingly important in Nazi occult circles, even the Hoerbigerians began to fall out among themselves. A meeting of them at Bad Pyrmont in 1936 resulted in a programme welcoming Himmler's patronage of the theory, demanding that it be used as the basis of future weather-forecasting, and calling for an 'intellectual Führer of World Ice' to be appointed and the exclusion of certain persons from the inner councils of the Hoerbigerian hierarchy.[17]

Soon accusations and counter-accusations were flying about among the fractious cosmologists. Various members were accused of being Jews, Freemasons, Catholics, Druids and confidence tricksters. The result of all this squabbling was that some members of the meeting were dismissed from their positions. One even ended up in a concentration camp – yet another occultist to suffer this fate in Nazi Germany.[18]

However, as a body of doctrine Hoerbigerianism remained as influential as ever. There continued to be a department of the Occult Bureau dedicated to forecasting the weather on the basis of the world ice theory. We shall now examine the way in which this occult weather-forecasting played a decisive part in losing the Germans the war on the Russian Front.

In June 1941 the Germans invaded Russia. By the middle of July, after the destruction of a number of Russian armies, German tanks were within range of Moscow. Then the Russians rallied; by October the winter had come to their assistance. From November onwards the Germans were fighting in sub-zero temperatures. Extraordinarily enough, they had not been issued with winter uniforms, and their sufferings from the weather – to say nothing of the determined Russian resistance – were enormous.

Why was it that Hitler had not allowed the German troops to be equipped with suitable clothing and equipment for the cold Russian winter? There are two main reasons, both of them occult. In the first place, Hitler was convinced that he had formed an alliance with the Frost Giants of Norse mythology. But the second and more decisive reason was that the weather-forecasters of the Occult Bureau, using Hoerbigerian ideas as the basis of their predictions, had promised a mild winter.[19]

It is certainly not the case that Hitler had anticipated a quick victory over the Russians. He had actually issued a memorandum calling for the subjugation of western Russia in around two years. And his orders to destroy the major Russian cities make it hard to see where his army was expected to find safe winter quarters. Hitler's extraordinary failure to provide his troops with the clothing and equipment they needed in order to survive a Russian winter makes no sense at all on any rational explanation. But since the Hoerbigerians had promised a mild winter – and Hitler, as we know from his conversations with Rauschning, was a convinced Hoerbigerian – suddenly his extraordinary blunder starts to make sense. So we see, not for the first time, that a major Nazi occult doctrine played a key role in losing them the war. Perhaps, considering how close they came to winning it in spite of their zany ideas, we should be grateful that they did give credence to and act upon such a huge cluster of impractical and crazy occult mythologizing.

8 Great Ball of Fire

The world ice theory was at the very centre of Nazi occult speculation, but it was by no means the only such cosmogony to attract the attention of Nazi occultists. Both Goering and a number of senior German naval officers subscribed to a theory which was, if possible, even more bizarre than that of Hoerbiger. This was the theory which became known as the 'hollow-earth' doctrine.

This theory originated as a speculation in 1692 by the astronomer Edmund Halley. Halley tried to explain the problem of magnetic fluctuation at the poles and suggested that if the earth was hollow, with solid outer layers, on the outermost of which human beings lived, it would explain the magnetic variations.[1]

Though Halley's idea was soon dismissed by orthodox scientists, Cotton Mather, the American clergyman who was largely responsible for the atrocities of the Salem witch trials, became converted to it. Through Mather's notoriety in the inquisitorial field his cosmological writings retained their interest; and, inevitably, through this interest the hollow-earth doctrine became widespread.[2]

Other figures who were attracted by the idea included the Scottish physicist Sir John Leslie, who decided that the earth contained two interior suns constantly revolving, and the Italian adventurer Casanova. But the man who really put the theory firmly on the map was John Symmes, another American Puritan. Through his reading of Mather, Symmes became converted to the hollow-earth doctrine and became an ardent propagandist for the idea.[3]

Symmes added to the basic idea the notion that the earth's poles contained openings which led to the interior of the hollow earth. He argued that these openings explained the phenomena described by the French astronomer Laplace, of an equatorial bulge and polar hollows. Symmes seized on these ideas and claimed that Laplace's hollows would lead directly to the centre of the earth.[4]

Another variant of the theory was put forward by Cyrus Teed, an American who preferred to be known as the Prophet Koresh. He produced a magazine called *The Flaming Sword*, in which he 'improved' upon Symmes's bizarre notions. Teed claimed boldly that the earth was hollow, but that we are not living on the outside of it. Instead, we are living in the interior of a hollow earth, with our own sun and the planets of the solar system being inside it too.[5]

A friend of Goering, Peter Bender, was a German fighter pilot during the First World War. He was shot down and spent the last two years of the war in a French prisoner-of-war camp. In the camp he read *The Flaming Sword* and became converted to Teed's hollow-earth theory. Just as Teed had 'improved' on Symmes, so Bender 'improved' upon Teed. He claimed that the universe was in fact extremely small, being entirely contained within the hollow earth. We live inside a globe at the centre of which is the sun. But points of light are constantly revolving around the sun. This continual effect of light leads us to believe in what Bender called 'the phantom universe'. Day and night are simply the result of the fact that the sun is on the other side of the phantom universe. Thus the hollow earth is the true centre of the cosmos, and the sun and other planets revolve around its central sphere. Astronomical observations are simply the result of our location relative to the position of the sun and planets within the hollow earth.[6]

When the Nazis came to power, Bender found a powerful friend in Goering. He was further helped by the astonishing number of high-ranking German naval officers who also believed in the hollow-earth doctrine. As a result of this, Bender was not merely able to avoid the usual fate of occultists under the Nazis – imprisonment in a concentration camp – but was even in a position to exert considerable influence on behalf of his theory. Through his friendship with Goering he was able to proselytize at will; through the many supporters in the navy he was able to attempt to have his theories put into practice in the same way as, say, Hoerbiger's followers did his.

One area of particular interest to the German navy was the problem of detecting enemy ships. Even reconnaissance planes can easily miss shipping when they are patrolling thousands of square miles of ocean. Radar, by contrast, has only a limited range of detection. If a way could be found of detecting the enemy vessels at a great distance, the hollow-earthists argued, it would enable the German navy to take action at once. And, they claimed, all that was needed was to aim radar detection apparatus at the heavens above. If this was done, they claimed, the waves would bounce back off the outside layer surrounding the centre and provide accurate signals of the positions of the objects at any given point on the surface of the hollow earth.

They baited their hook with an argument designed to provide empirical evidence for the truth of the hollow-earth theory. The Prophet Koresh, they explained, had conducted an experiment in Florida with an instrument known as a rectilineator. He had used this to trace a straight line from the coast of Florida until it had disappeared into the sea. This proved, they said, that sea level must be higher than land level. But this could only be true if we lived on the inside of a hollow earth.[7]

For some five years Bender and his followers argued with passionate determination for their hollow-earth doctrine. With Goering's patronage behind them, and strong support in the navy, they were making sufficient progress among occult-inclined Nazis for their main rivals, the Hoerbigerians, to become alarmed. So concerned were they, particularly at the progress Bender's ideas were making in the navy and air force, that they went right to the top in their attempt to stop them. They appealed to Hitler for a complete ban on all writing or speaking on behalf of the hollow-earth theory. Hoerbiger's world ice theory, they complained, provided a complete explanation of cosmogony. It was impossible for it to be true and the hollow-earth theory not to be false. And, they argued, since the world ice theory was correct, surely the answer was plain? They appealed to Hitler to suppress the hollow-earth theory.

But the Hoerbigerians had underestimated the extent of Hitler's willingness to entertain mutually incompatible theories.

He replied to the demands that he should choose between them as follows: 'Our conception of the world need not be coherent. They may both be right.'[8]

Although the Hoerbigerians had no success with Hitler, they had more luck with Rosenberg. At times Rosenberg could be almost rational by the standards of the Nazi leadership. His own sympathies lay with neither theory, but while he regarded Hoerbiger's ideas as unlikely, Bender's struck him as both ludicrous and impossible. When in 1938 a hollow-earth theorist called Johannes Lang applied for permission to give a lecture on Koresh's hollow-world doctrine, Rosenberg managed to discover that Lang was also an amateur astrologer who had been unwise enough once to publish a horoscope of Hitler. As we have seen, this was a serious offence in Nazi Germany.

Using this as a lever, Rosenberg moved against both Lang and other hollow-earth theorists. His official position was that the theory was 'a completely unscientific explanation of outer space'. But Rosenberg took care to make the real nature of Lang's offence known. Although in itself it did not implicate other hollow-earth theorists, inevitably they were tarred with the same brush.[9]

In spite of this setback, Bender retained his influence in the navy and air force. Nor were the occult possibilities of his doctrine missed by the members of the Vril Society, to which many Nazis were at least sympathetic. The Vril Society believed that the Secret Chiefs, beings far in advance of ordinary mortals, lived underground, in openings found at various points in the earth. But the Vril Society had made contact with the underground masters and was busy trying to realize powers on earth.

Initiates of the Vril Society apparently spent much of their time looking at an apple which had been cut in half. This was meant to aid meditation and increase *vril* power through intense mental concentration. They believed that *vril*, the energy of life, was the source of all power in the world. Whoever managed to control *vril*-power would become master of the earth. The lords of the underground world lived in the inside of the hollow earth.[10]

This powerful Nazi occult society decided to add its own considerable weight to the already powerful backing of the navy and air force. Although Hoerbigerianism was still the more widely supported occult cosmology among Nazis, the hollow-earth theory had sufficient support to survive the Lang fiasco and continue its propagandizing.

There was an additional argument which Bender and his followers put forward in favour of their theory. Hoerbiger's theory was unable to provide an explanation of various scientific paradoxes which only seemed to make sense on the assumption that Einstein's theory of relativity was true. But Einstein was a Jew, and relativity could therefore not possibly be true. The Hoerbigerians could offer no alternative explanation; but the hollow-earth theorists could.

Einstein showed that light is a series of particles which shrink along the path they travel. He also showed that it was a form of energy, and that energy was relative to the speed of light. Michelson and Morley had shown that the speed of light is the same whether it travels in the same direction as the rotation of the earth or if it travels at right-angles to the orbit. Hoerbiger's followers had no answer to this; but Bender did. He claimed that, since the earth was hollow, it does not move. It is the fixed centre of the entire universe. Only the sun and moon really exist besides the hollow earth, the rest of observed planetary and stellar bodies belonging to the phantom universe. Since the earth does not move, of course it makes no different in which direction the particles of light travel. At the time there was no empirical or experimental verification of Einstein's theory. We had to wait for the atom bomb before that happened. Until then, Bender's theory, crazy as it was, fitted the facts just as much as Einstein's. And Bender was an Aryan, so his theory had to be preferred.[11]

This line of reasoning was enough to convince many people who wanted to find a purely Aryan explanation. It was certainly enough for the German navy, which was in any case steeped in every conceivable variety of occultism. On the outbreak of war, they saw their chance at last. It did not come at once, but by 1942 Bender had managed to persuade the German government to fund an expedition to prove the truth of the hollow-earth theory. Not only Goering but also Himmler and Hitler gave their approval for this bizarre expedition in the middle of the war. Leading German experts in the field of radar were ordered to take part in this expedition, and the party was led by Dr Heinz Fischer, an expert on infra-red rays.

The expedition landed on the island of Rügen, in the Baltic. In spite of the extreme scarcity of radar equipment, the party was equipped with the most up-to-date and sophisticated instruments. On arrival at Rügen, Fischer and his team set up the equipment and directed the radar towards the sky at an angle of forty-five degrees. It remained in that position for several days.

The object of the expedition was twofold. First, to show that the reflection of radar rays in a straight line could give an image of any point within the sphere of the hollow earth. The second objective was to use the reflection to get an image of the British navy, based at Scapa Flow. The rationale behind this was that the concave 'curvature of the earth would facilitate long-distance observations by means of infra-red rays, which are less curved than visible rays'.

After a considerable amount of time, energy and equipment had been spent on this attempt to prove the truth of the hollow-earth theory, Fischer and his team had to give it up as a failure. Had he been vindicated, Bender would have been honoured by the Nazis; but, as he had been decisively disproved, his influence came to an abrupt end. Even Goering could not prevent him from being thrown into a concentration camp, along with many of his most ardent disciples. In spite of the hollow-earthists' frantic claims that the radar equipment must have 'malfunctioned', the theory was henceforth officially banned in Nazi Germany. Some managed to survive the camps and began proselytizing again after the war; but most died in the camps. Fischer's comment on the whole thing, admittedly after the war had ended, was: 'The Nazis forced me to do crazy things which hindered me considerably in my researches.' But perhaps we should be grateful that they did, for Fischer went on to help develop the H-bomb in the United States.[12]

Bender's theory did not die with him entirely, but it was never again to exercise any influence on government policy. It survives nowadays only on the farther fringes of fundamentalist Christianity and among flying-saucer enthusiasts, many of whom firmly believe that 'extra-terrestrials' actually come from inside the hollow earth. But of the Nazis and their involvement with the phenomenon of flying saucers, we shall be writing in another chapter of this book.

9 The Tibetan Connection

Tibet has always been a land of mystery and magic. To many Westerners it has been regarded as a special country, a land of lamas and yogis and miracle-workers with spiritual powers unmatched anywhere else. Although its reputation as a sacred land is very old indeed, the modern interest in Tibet among occultists dates back largely to the days of Madame Blavatsky and her Theosophical Society.

This society became enormously popular in the late nineteenth and early twentieth century. Many Nazis were keen Theosophists, and many also belonged to another secret tradition derived from Tibet. To this latter group the sinister Haushofer belonged.[1] Blavatsky claimed that she received her 'secret doctrine' from masters who dwelt in Tibet. These masters were superhuman beings, who from time to time intervened to enlighten humanity through chosen mortal instruments.

There were four main occult groupings within Tibet: the Yellow Caps, or orthodox Buddhists, represented by the Dalai Lama; the followers of the Apostolic Succession, who believe in an unbroken line of gurus possessed of spiritual wisdom; the Red Caps, best known as powerful magicians and occultists; and the Black Caps, monastic orders of non-Buddhist Tibetans. The followers of the Apostolic Succession do not believe in God; they speak instead of a 'primordial man'. The feminine principle in nature is spoken of as wisdom; instead of a belief in personal immortality, reincarnation is adopted as the preferred explanation. There is no God, only the 'law of cause and effect'. In Tibetan initiation ceremonies, a psychic process designed to transmit power to the initiate, is adopted. The master gives off a subtle energy, which the disciple 'draws off' during the ceremony and is 'endowed with power'. Meditation, telepathy, concentration and various physically extraordinary phenomena can result from this training and initiation.[2]

The name given by Tibetan adepts to their paradise is Shamballah. The legend of Shamballah lies behind *Lost Horizon*, James Hilton's extraordinary novel about a Himalayan paradise.

All the Far Eastern traditions agree that Shamballah was the origin and source of a vast body of occult wisdom, greater than any other place on earth. The Shamballic tradition in Tibet is closely linked to the Indian Tantric religious systems, which emphasize the role of sexual magic and are known by the sinister nickname, 'the Left-Hand Path'.[3]

According to the myth, Shamballah is a city hidden among mountains, barred in addition by a great lake, and only approachable through a narrow opening in a hard-to-find cave. In the heart of the city is a vast tower, the palace of the king of Shamballah. But the city stretches both up and down; it includes a vast network of underground caves and tunnels, spreading out all over the world. This underground realm within Shamballah is called Agarthi, which means 'inaccessible'.

The ruler of Agarthi was 'the King of the World', who was in direct touch with a supreme higher being and also governed the world by exerting telepathic and psychic powers over other rulers on the surface of the earth. From time to time he actually emerged and met with human agents, instructing them on how to carry out his wishes for the world.

In 1890 the King of the World is said to have uttered a series of prophecies about the next fifty years of world history. He predicted a series of bloody wars and revolutions, after which the people of Agarthi would come up to the surface of the earth and take over.[4]

Not surprisingly, many occult-inclined politicians were fascinated by the possibilities of this legend. One of the first to seek to turn the powers of Shamballah and Agarthi to his own advantage was the mad Russian, Ungern-Sternberg. After the Russian Revolution he became active in the White Army forces of Koltchak in Siberia, and when the Bolsheviks defeated

Koltchak, Ungern-Sternberg escaped into Mongolia, with quite a few men and a fair amount of equipment. He installed himself in the Mongolian capital, proclaiming himself king, and becoming a convert to Lamaism. He made extensive use of prophecy and fortune-telling, predicting amongst other things the exact date of his own death. He set up an 'Order of Military Buddhists', which was enjoined to celibacy and to the idea of sinning in order to be able to expiate the sin. He had a vision of an empire stretching from Mongolia to Lake Baikal, allied to a tsarist Russia and a monarchist China. None of these dreams came to pass: instead, Ungern-Sternberg, after a series of bloody persecutions directed particularly against the Jews, rode off to defeat and death at the hands of the Red Army on an insane attempt to reconquer Siberia.[5]

Ungern-Sternberg's exploits were described by another White Russian, Ossendowski. Ossendowski also escaped from the Bolsheviks and fled into Mongolia, where he met the mad despot. Ossendowski believed that the King of the World would bring about a new age, sweeping aside the hated Bolsheviks in Russia and spreading the gospel of Agarthi across the Western world. For Ossendowski, the centre of the king's power was Agarthi, whose subterranean radiance dispersed itself out across the world. The Tashi Lama had been the King of the World in a previous incarnation. Many Tibetans expected him to return as the long-expected Buddhist Maitreya, the new Buddha.[6]

In 1923, a number of fateful 'coincidences' happened. In the first place, Hitler made his bungled Munich *putsch*. That same year, Moeller van den Bruck published his book *The Third Reich*. In the very same year, a German called Mühle founded an occult-political movement which proclaimed the imminent advent of a thousand-year Reich. Another one was the beginning of a series of travels by one of the twentieth century's outstanding white magicians, Nicholas Roerich. And the final 'coincidence' was that the Tashi Lama was forced to leave his monastery and escape into Mongolia. There he met men who had been deeply influenced by Ungern-Sternberg's teachings, and were ready to listen to the Tashi Lama when he made similar pronouncements. Nor were there doubters when he claimed that he was in direct touch with the underground hierarchy of Shamballah. We shall deal with Roerich's exploits soon; but for now we shall consider the activities of the Tashi Lama.[7]

In the first place, he spoke of a great war, 'the War of Chang Shamballah'. The warriors of Shamballah would soon rise and take possession of the whole earth. The King of the World was waiting for the right moment to strike, but he would come. When he did come again, he would restore power to Asia and end the powers of the white race for ever.[8]

The Shamballah/Agarthi myths entered Nazism, like many of its occult doctrines, through the influence of Haushofer. The mentor of Hitler had learned his powers through his membership of a Japanese secret society called the Order of the Green Dragon, which he had joined in Japan, though its origins were Tibetan.[9]

One member of the Green Dragon tried to control the various forces – liquid, electrical, gaseous, metallic etc. – in the human body. They also wanted to gain power over time. One of their most important rituals was that designed to control the vital energy within plants. By a process of magical concentration the initiate was supposed to be able to make a blossom appear within a few minutes. Haushofer was one of only three Europeans who have ever been permitted to join the Green Dragons. In the event of failure in his mission, the member of the order is required to commit ritual suicide; and, after the failure of the Nazi 'mission', that is exactly what Haushofer did.[10]

The ideas of Haushofer and his Vril Society emanated from a variety of sources, but was entirely composed of Satanists. Its membership included Japanese, Indians, Turks, Sinhalese and Tibetans, as well as Germans. The Vril Society was dedicated to research into Atlantis, the origins of the Aryan race and the reawakening of the magical powers which lay dormant within those of Aryan blood. This research, so the members believed, would enable initiates to become possessed of superhuman powers, of the same kind and stature as those enjoyed by the King of the World.[11]

In the cosmology of the Vril Society, the earth itself is a living organism, a vast psychic consciousness to which every single aspect of inner and outer life belongs in a relationship of mutual interdependence. The breathing of the subtle body of the earth is the breath of life which guides and shapes the whole process of evolution upon the planet. In the year 1909, they believed, the date at which a new cycle in human evolution began, the rebirth of magical powers would usher in a new era in human history. And 1909 was the very year in which Hitler had first stood in the Treasure House at Vienna and gazed so longingly upon the Spear of Destiny.[12]

Hitler became an initiative of the Vril Society himself and absorbed its teachings eagerly. He believed that in the very near future the newly enlightened race of Aryan supermen would be able to travel in time, both backwards and forwards. As well as recovering the primitive history of the race, they would be able to glimpse the future destiny of humanity. 'What today is known as history,' Hitler said, 'we will abolish altogether.' Hitler also believed that this process would lead to the opening of what he called 'the Cyclops Eye', which lived in the pineal gland and would unlock forever all the secrets of time. In future, men would perceive the world psychically as easily as they now did through their physical eyes.[13]

As Hitler himself put it:

> Creation is not yet completed. Man must pass through many further stages of metamorphosis. Post-Atlantean man is already in a state of degeneration and decline, barely able to survive. All creative forces will be concentrated in a new species. The two types of man, the old and the new, will evolve rapidly in differnt directions. One will disappear from the face of the earth, the other will flourish. This is the real motive behind the National Socialist Movement! I am founding an Order. It is from there that the final stage in human mutation will emerge – the MAN-GOD![14]

Hitler, like Haushofer, believed that the Secret Chiefs were based in Tibet. In the beginning, so the Vril Society taught, men were simply mirror-images of the gods. Then a hierarchy of powers arose, who tried to persuade man to resist the plans of the 'angelic orders'. These spirits became known collectively as Lucifer, and operated on a psychic level. They cut the 'umbilical cord' between people and the gods, leaving humanity rudderless and open to their suggestions. But then a second process of development took place, within the material world, to which another group of spirits from the Satanic realm turned their attention. These second group of spirits were collectively known as Ahriman. Their job was to cut people off completely from all contact with the higher levels of consciousness, and to persuade them that the three-dimensional world of matter which they inhabited was the only reality.[15]

According to the Vril Society, after the fall of Thule its survivors migrated eastwards, through Europe and Asia, until at last they settled in Tibet. These survivors of the magical elite of Thule lived in two caves underneath the mountains, where they pursued their magical activities. After 5,000 years the 'good' oracle died out, and only the black magicians were left to spread their teachings all over Tibet. Their shrines continued until the Chinese invasion in 1959, when the Communists made the suppression of Tibetan Lamaism their first priority.[16]

By the beginning of the twentieth century, Tibet had become a sacred land to many Western occultists. The members of the Thule group and the Vril Society both spoke of two secret orders following left- and right-hand paths respectively. The oracle of Agarthi sought to create false leadership in all nations of the world – which must have pleased the Nazis. The oracle of Shamballah tried to promote materialism and keep men in ignorance of their true spiritual nature and destiny.[17]

Through the urgings of Haushofer and other members of the Vril Society, the Nazis sent out a whole series of expeditions to Tibet. Every year from 1926 to 1942 the Germans sent out parties which contacted Tibetan initiates with the firm intention of getting them to help the Nazis in their aims of the occult subjugation of the rest of the world.[18]

In 1929, three years after the Nazis had first made contact with the monks of Agarthi and Shamballah, a Tibetan colony was established in Germany, with branches in Berlin, Nuremberg and Munich. Apparently, however, only the monks of Agarthi were willing to help the Nazis. The initiates of Shamballah preferred to work through the Freemasons. The monks from Agarthi were known in Germany as 'The Society of Green Men', because of their strong links – for hundreds of years – with the Green Dragon Society of Japan, to which Haushofer himself belonged. Indeed seven members of the society joined up with the German-based group.[19]

In Berlin, Hitler met regularly with the leader of the Tibetan community, a monk notable for his feats of clairvoyance and precognition. He was nicknamed 'the man with the green gloves', and on three separate occasions correctly predicted, in the press, the precise number of Nazi deputies elected to the German Parliament. He also foretold the exact date when Hitler would become leader of Germany, and even the date when the Second World War would begin.[20] This level of successful prediction soon attracted wide interest among the Nazi occultists. Himmler, as well as Hitler, became deeply interested in Tibetan Lamaism. He set up an occult training college at the Berlin section and ordered members of the SS leadership to attend courses there, especially in magic. As a result of his contacts with the group, Himmler set up the Nazi Occult Bureau. This incorporated into one organization the Thule group, the Vril Society and the German branch of the Ordo Templi Orientis (OTO) – Aleister Crowley's magical order.[21]

The Nazi Party anthem was inspired by Horst Wessel, a keen Hoerbigerian who had helped to organize the Storm-Troopers in the 1920s, and in 1926 was shot dead by the Communists. A German poet and occultist called Ewers wrote a song, 'The Horst Wessel Hymn', which became the theme song and sacred anthem of the Nazi Party. And Ewers openly said that he joined the Nazis because he saw it as 'the strongest expression of the Powers of Darkness'.[22]

The founders of the Nazi Party comprised two men, who soon recruited others. But with the decision of Hitler to join the party, it acquired member number seven. The seven founders of Nazism, then dreamed of 'changing life on Earth'. Each man believed that he was in direct league with the 'Powers of Darkness'. Even the magical oath which bound them together was one derived from Tibetan sources. The Norse god Thor was supposed to have been a survivor of the ruins of Thule, and come from Tibet through the Gobi Desert into Europe.

Surprisingly, certain rumours of Nazi occult activity began to filter slowly out of Germany. John Buchan, in his novel *A Prince of the Captivity*, warned of the dangers of Nazism, in particular its combination of political power with the dark workings of Satanism. Kipling, who had used the swastika for years as his own personal symbol, instructed his publishers to remove it from the covers of his books. And Saint-George Saunders published two remarkable books in which he said openly that the source of Nazi Satanic activities was Tibet.[23]

Until 1942 both the Tibetan magicians and Haushofer himself were held in high regard by Hitler. Then, ironically, in the same year that the hollow-earth experiments were proved unsuccessful, the Russian broke the back of the German army at Stalingrad. From then on Hitler no longer believed in the magic of Agarthi. Haushofer's own influence over Hitler also declined, being replaced by that of the even more sinister figure Friedrich Hielscher. This man belonged to a still higher order of black magicians than Haushofer, and had attained an even more exalted degree of initiations. Even Himmler was afraid of him, and described him as the most powerful man in Germany after Hitler. Under Hielscher's cold Satanic direction, Hitler turned from the unsystematic harassment and murder of individual Jews to the full horror of the Final Solution.[24]

Another of the astonishing 'coincidences' which keep cropping up throughout our story concerns the extraordinary exploits of Nicholas Roerich. Between 1923 and 1928 Roerich went on a series of travels throughout central Asia, accompanied by his son George. In 1926 – the same year that the Nazis sent their first expedition to Tibet – Roerich was also in that country. He spoke with many Lamas and other Tibetan occultists and mystics. They spoke of the imminent arrival of the Maitreya, the Buddhist Messiah, and imparted to Roerich the spiritual meaning of Altai. It seems that, among other things, the chief mountain of the Altai range was regarded as the dwelling-place of the gods. The Bear and Orion were singled out as being constellations associated with the esoteric wisdom of Altai. The seven stars were seen as the seven Wise Ones, and were also associated with the Mongol legend of Gesar, the Mongol Maitreya, despite his being a warrior rather than a sage. And Gesar was always linked in legend with the Tibetan stories of Shamballah. Beluka, the principal mountain in the Altai range, has also been put forward as the possible origin of the legend of Mount Merou, abode of the gods. And from Tibet, from the Altai range, civilization gradually began to spread outwards.

Both black and white magic are possible; one can always choose whether to follow the left- or the right-hand path. But magic in itself is morally neutral. Tibet held within itself both black and white magicians, and it was, of course, those initiates dedicated to the dark powers of evil who helped Hitler and the Nazis. But other powers existed in Tibet as well, and Roerich, among others, made contact with them.

Roerich himself said, in his book *The Heart of Asia*, that Shamballah was the fountain and crown of all true wisdom. 'If you wish to understand Asia and to approach her as a welcome guest,' he wrote, 'you must meet your host with the most sacred word – Shambhala.'[25] Roerich and his expedition were based in the Himalayas and had extensive contacts with wise men in Tibet. Roerich became a vehicle of transmission for a Mahatma Morya, who taught a system of Agni Yoga, based on the Kundalini power.[26] Roerich states that a Lama passed through an underground passage in order to reach a sacred place. And the borders of the 'hidden land' were marked out carefully with occult symbols.

Among the huge snow-capped mountains of Tibet, Roerich tells us, there lurk, as if waiting for the discovery of one who truly seeks, hidden valleys of astonishing beauty and pulsating with life. Hot springs feed lush vegetation among the secret valleys, surrounded by impenetrable walls of rock and snow and ice. Sometimes the guardians of these valleys could be seen, and were often described as 'snowmen'. Could this, we wonder, be the true origin of the Yeti legend? It is surely significant that one of Roerich's paintings features a 'snow maiden', clasping a bow in her hand as she stands among rocks and snow, yet almost naked. Roerich also draws attention to the vast labyrinth of caves and underground passages that exist in Tibet and the Himalayas. 'From these caves,' he says, 'subterranean passages proceed far below Kinchinjunga. Some have even seen the stone door which has never been opened, because the date has not arrived. The deep passages proceed to the splendid valley.'[27]

The valley of which Roerich speaks is, of course, the valley of Shamballah. According to reports by both Roerich and Ossendowski, the underground tunnels of Shamballah were hundreds of kilometres long. Ossendowski also spoke of 'strange cars' which hurried along these underground tunnels.[28]

In *The Heart of Asia* Roerich speaks of the strange experiences of a Chinese doctor who travelled through the Gobi Desert and 'severe uplands' to the valley of Shamballah. He found there a school of yogis intent on studying the ancient wisdom of mankind. The account the doctor gave struck Roerich as being similar in most respects to his own descriptions of Shamballah. The doctor described many 'scientific wonders' and experiments in telepathy, psychical use of the will and the influence of psychic and magical powers over distances.[29]

Ossendowski claimed that the network of caves and tunnels housed the remnants of the surviving Atlantean elite. They apparently lit their subterranean fastnesses by some kind of artificial light. 'In underground caves,' he said, 'there exists a peculiar light which affords growth to the grains and vegetables and long life without disease to the people.'[30]

The Tibetans claimed that the enlightened ones enjoyed transcendental powers, which gave them dominion over space, time and matter. They could make their body any size or height they chose, and could materialize in any place they wished. Five perfect men were said to preside over the destiny of the world. Once a year they met together in a Himalayan cave to decide on the destiny of the planet. Under these enlightened ones were the hundreds of initiates who made up the inhabitants of Shamballah.[31]

According to George Roerich, Nicholas's son, who accompanied him on his series of expeditions, for centuries the Tibetan Lamas have tried to stay in constant contact with the king of Shamballah. The present Dalai Lama's brother refers to the existence of Shamballah as a simple fact of experience. And the Mahatma Morya, speaking through Nicholas Roerich, calls Shamballah 'the city of science'. He adds the following:

> In our community one can meet many nationalities and different professions. The geographer can be set at ease. We do occupy a definite place on the earth. The conspirator can be comforted; in various parts of the world we have a sufficient quantity of co-workers.[32]

But this was written when the shadow of Nazi black magic was passing across the world. Who were these co-workers? To judge from Roerich himself, they were benevolent; but it seems clear that there were also other, darker currents among the initiates of Tibet. And Roerich himself may even have met some in his travels. But he makes, in a calm, factual manner, the astonishing statement: 'We know that some high lamas went to Shambhala, how along their way they saw the customary physical things. Moreover, we ourselves have seen a white frontier post of one of the three posts of Shambhala.'[33] And Roerich also tells us that the search for Shamballah and communion with its king has been the true goal of all followers of the Kalachakra, or Tantric path.

In 1945 the war was at last coming to its inevitable end. Germany had been defeated, and only small pockets of determined resistance to the Allied advance remained. In Berlin itself, Russian soldiers fought hand-to-hand with German youths; but as they overcame the last flickers of resistance, in the eastern quarters of the city, a strange sight met their eyes. To their astonishment the Russians came across large numbers of Tibetan corpses. They were dressed in German uniform, but had no badges or insignia of rank. In neat, orderly rows they lay upon the ground, each one with a ritual knife which had pierced their stomachs. Rather than surrender to the Russians and add further to their disgrace, they had chosen to commit ritual suicide.[34] Haushofer also followed the Tibetans into ritual *hara-kiri*, in accordance with the oath he had sworn on joining the Japanese Green Dragon Society. He first killed his wife and then himself. No cross or gravestone marks the place where Haushofer, initiate of evil, lies buried. Whatever secrets he had, died with him.[35]

One final twist to the tale of Tibet and Shamballah and their association with the Nazis is that a number of top Party members, including Martin Bormann, are said to have escaped from the doomed ruins of Berlin through secret underground passages and travelled by them as far as South America. The curious thing is that there really are traditions of secret tunnels in South America, and that the legends link them with Europe and even Shamballah and Agarthi themselves.[36] Amazing as it seems, the Nazis may actually have succeeded in making their way through the underground passages to Agarthi and Shamballah. Who knows what other forces of light or darkness may even now be dwelling deep within the hidden recesses of the earth?

10 The Nazis and Flying Saucers

This chapter may well be the strangest in the whole of this book. Once again it brings us to Tibet, and once again Roerich is involved in our investigations.

There is no doubt that most flying-saucer experiences are either mistaken sightings of natural phenomena, hysterical people hallucinating or downright lies. And yet there are two cases which do not quite seem to fit the normal explanations. The first is the famous 'Tungus event', when in 1908, over Siberia – a land steeped in Shamanism, and with strong magical links with Tibet and Mongolia – a most curious explosion occurred. A huge, bright object hurried across the sky at breathtaking speed, and was seen over an enormous area of Siberia. The object suddenly exploded in mid-air, the sound being heard 500 miles away. A pillar of fire and cloud shot into the air, which wiped out whole herds of reindeer and two villages in the vicinity. Now the strange thing about the Tungus explosion is that it could not possibly have been a meteorite. The party of Russian scientists who went to investigate it found no crater, nor any sign of any collision, nor any fragments of meteorite. As far as twenty miles around the site, the forests had been flattened. The trees which had fallen bore scorch marks, and later, evidence of radioactivity in the soil and tree-trunks was detected. All the evidence would suggest to a modern observer an atomic explosion. And yet – there were no atom bombs on earth in 1908. What is more, the explosion was by air only a few minutes away from the Altai mountain range. Most of the Russian scientists seemed to conclude that it was an atomic-powered spaceship which blew up in mid-air. The

German rocket scientist Willy Ley, who escaped from the Nazis in 1933, also admits that the Tungus event shows all the signs of an atomic explosion. But Ley, a rationalist who had seen enough of Nazi irrationality at work to terrify him, did not want to entertain the hypothesis that the object was an alien spaceship. Instead, he suggests that the explosion was of a meteor made of anti-matter. At this late stage it is obviously impossible to decide conclusively one way or another. Nevertheless, it is an important and problematic case, for the Tungus event left clear physical consequences, including the devastation of a wide area and the deaths of many people and animals. However, the explanation for it cannot be the same as that for the flying-saucer sighting described by Roerich, for which I shall offer a satisfactory explanation in due course. But the association with the Altai mountains is suggestive and significant. Ley's anti-matter looks the most likely answer; but could the underground world of Agarthi be somehow involved with a universe of anti-matter?[1]

Roerich spoke of a Tibetan legend of a black stone, a huge meteor which had once fallen upon Shamballah. He was engaged in restoring the stone – a fragment of the now lost original – to its original setting. This stone was apparently one of peculiar holiness, and Roerich saw it as the key to his entire mission in central Asia, and Tibet in particular.

In the summer of 1927 Roerich and his expedition were camped in a valley between Tibet and Mongolia. There, Roerich built a shrine, a 'stately white structure' which he dedicated to Shamballah. He wrote the following cryptic note regarding this act of consecration in his diary. 'On July 20th directions of the utmost importance reached us. They are difficult to execute but they may lead to certain results. No one in the caravan as yet suspects our immediate programme.'[2]

What on earth is Roerich talking about so mysteriously here? Who gave him his mysterious directions? And what precisely were they? Surely the mere building of a shrine, however sacred, could not be enough to justify such exaggerated secrecy? But its dedication to Shamballah may be extremely significant. It may be that Roerich had made direct contact with intelligences from the Shamballah centre, who had charged him with the accomplishment of certain tasks – we shall never know which ones. Bearing in mind the nature of the knowledge which

Shamballah was said to possess, perhaps Roerich felt there were good reasons for his secrecy. Especially if black magicians were also busily at work on their own perverted schemes.

He finished the main body of the shrine, and invited a group of Lamas and other dignitaries to witness its consecration. Then he wrote another baffling entry in his diary. 'I am going joyously into the battle. *Lapis exilis* – the wandering stone. Yesterday the Buriats foretold something impending. I am sending the best currents for the happy decision of the works.' The shrine was finished in August, and the Elder Lama of Tsaidam consecrated it.[3]

On 5 August Roerich springs another surprise on his readers.

> Something remarkable! [he begins] In the morning some of our caravaneers noticed a remarkably big black eagle flying over us. Seven of us began to watch this unusual bird. At this moment another of our caravaneers shouted, 'There is something far above the bird.' We all saw something big and shiny reflecting the sun, like a huge oval moving at great speed. Crossing our camp the thing changed direction from south to south-west. And we saw how it disappeared in the intense blue sky. We even had time to take our field glasses and saw quite distinctly an oval form with shiny surface, one side of which was brilliant from the sun.[4]

In another book, Roerich again speaks of his strange sighting.

> A sunny, unclouded morning – the blue sky is brilliant. Over our camp flies a huge, dark vulture. Our Mongols and we watch it. Suddenly one of the Buriat lamas points into the blue sky. 'What is that? A white balloon? An aeroplane?' We notice something shiny, flying very high from the north-east to the south. We bring three powerful field glasses from the tents and watch the huge spheroid body shining against the sun, clearly visible against the blue sky and moving very fast. Afterwards we see that it sharply changes its direction from south to south-west and disappears behind the snow-peaked Humboldt Chain.[5]

There is almost too much food for thought here. In the first place, the black eagle was the symbol of imperial Germany. Admittedly, the second book calls it a vulture, but it may be a significant symbol even so. Secondly, the phrase '*lapis exilis*' strongly suggests, and may even be a coded expression for '*lapis excellis*', the 'precious stone'. This stone is often associated with the grail legends, and so once again we trace a possible occult significance. And Hitler and Himmler were both obsessively interested in the grail legends. Could there be an echo of this, here in the heart of the country which both Roerich and the Nazis viewed as the source of all wisdom?

But the real surprise is in what can only be described as a classic flying-saucer vision. In the first place, the sky was cloudless. There is no possibility of poor visibility having played tricks on the perceptions of the expedition party. Secondly, they were even able to observe the object through field glasses. Not only did this give them a better look at the phenomenon, but it also means that the object must have been moving at a speed which enabled them the time to get binoculars from their tents and observe the object more closely. The change of direction is also stated to be 'sharp' – another characteristic of flying-saucer reports.

Now Roerich was perfectly familiar with airships and aeroplanes. Had the object in question resembled either, he would certainly have made it clear. Instead he describes the shape of the object as 'spheroid'. And no known flying-machine can turn sharply without killing its crew, because of the problem of inertia. The technology for such a craft does not exist now, much less in 1927.

Nor was Roerich, unlike many UFO observers, either a crank or a fool. He was a man of wide learning and a highly gifted painter who had already sketched much of what he had seen during his central Asian travels. The sighting also appeared to six other people among his company who were watching the black bird along with Roerich himself. So, at the very least, we are talking about mass hallucination, which is always a difficult position to argue for. Nor can we say that he saw a flying saucer because he was looking for one. For Roerich's sighting happened exactly twenty years before the first 'chain of saucer-like objects' was seen by Kenneth Arnold. It was Arnold who coined the term 'flying saucer', and before him no one had thought about them at all. How, then, could Roerich have seen a flying saucer when neither the concept nor the term had even been invented yet? And why should mass hallucination produce a sighting of something that no one had expected to see? After

Arnold, people started seeing saucers with monotonous regularity; but in 1927 there was no such tradition. And if the Lamas were responsible, why should they – in a country where neither airships nor aeroplanes existed – choose to make Roerich see a flying-saucer image? And Arnold did not know about Roerich or his work, so how is it that his sighting should be so remarkably similar to Roerich's?

This sighting is surely the most impressive of all the various flying-saucer visions. Significantly, it was seen in Tibet, and coming from the direction of the Altai mountains. What is more, it came at the very time when Roerich had erected his shrine to Shamballah.

Roerich, in his second account, tells us himself that the Lamas who were with him described the saucer as 'the sign of Shambhala'. He also says that he spoke of his vision with another Lama who was not present, but who gave the impression that he knew more about it than he was prepared to reveal. 'Something shiny and beautiful,' Roerich said, had flown south over his camp. Asked by the Lama if he had smelt incense like that which came from temples, Roerich agreed that he had smelt just such a perfume.

> Ah [the Lama told him], you are guarded by Shambhala. The huge black vulture is your enemy, who is eager to destroy your work, but the protecting force from Shambhala follows you in this radiant form of matter. This force is always near you, but you cannot always perceive it. Sometimes only, it is manifested for strengthening and directing you. Did you notice the direction in which this sphere moved? You must follow the same direction. You mentioned to me the sacred call – Kaligiya! When some one hears this imperative call, he must know that the way to Shambhala is open to him. He must remember when he was called, because from that time evermore, he is closely assisted by the Blessed Rigden Jye-po [the legendary king of Shamballah]. Only you must know and realise the manner in which people are helped because often people repel the help which is sent.[6]

The help, then, which Roerich expected, was to come from Shamballah itself, and the object which he had seen, coming from the Altai mountain range, clearly places Shamballah in a particular time and place. Acting on his instructions, Roerich packed up his camp and headed south-south-west across Tibet.

But no sign or revelation followed him, or if one did it never saw the light of day in his books. Unless, of course, that tantalizing reference to seeing 'the white frontier post of one of the three posts of Shambhala' can be taken to imply that he did, in fact, reach his goal and make contact with Shamballah.[7]

Now it is part of Lamaist teaching that the mind has the power to create 'tulpas', or 'thought-forms'. Men and women can actually project mental images of people and objects which then objectify themselves on the physical level. 'Matter is a development of thought, crystallized mental energy,' as one source on Tibetan Buddhism informs us.[8] And the words of the Lama who told Roerich what his vision meant certainly imply that his saucer was a thought-form sent from Shamballah for Roerich's own enlightenment. Alexandra David-Neel, in her book *With Mystics and Magicians in Tibet*, recounts how

> Tibetan magicians relate cases in which the tulpa is sent to fulfil a mission, but does not come back and pursues its peregrinations as a half-conscious, dangerously mischievous puppet. The same thing, it is said, may happen when the maker of the tulpa dies before having dissolved it.[9]

Could it be, we wonder, that whoever projected the flying-saucer tulpa for Roerich's benefit may have sent out such a powerful thought-form that he could no longer control it? Or did the unknown adept die before he had time to dissolve it again? For whatever reason, twenty years after Roerich's sighting, flying-saucer mania hit the world.[10]

Who or what was behind the projection of such a tulpa, moreover? Roerich was deeply sympathetic to Soviet Communism, and for this reason, among others, was considered to be an occultist hostile to the Nazis. Did they project the image of a black bird – the bird which the Lama said was the sign of Roerich's enemy who was seeking to destroy him? Now Roerich was considered by his friends and disciples to be in direct contact with the Masters, and there are signs in his writings that he also felt this to have been the case. He also believed that the Masters had a close and abiding relationship with Shamballah, to which sacred place Roerich built his shrine in the desolate regions of Tibet. And it was this act of devotion which led to Roerich's sighting of the first flying saucer. Clearly, then, the tulpa must probably be considered to be a projection either from Shamballah itself, or from someone or something closely connected with it.[11]

What is particularly significant about Roerich's sighting is the date: 1927. This was the second year running that a Nazi expedition to Tibet had been sent to make contact with the black magicians of Agarthi. The black bird, the mention of a sacred stone, the curious words *lapis exilis* (which suggest the grail stone), and the fact that the Lamas spoke of it as 'the sign of Shambhala', all argue in favour of some powerful occult involvement by both pro- and anti-Nazi groups within Tibet. Did the initiates of Shamballah sense that the Nazi threat to civilization was so strong that only the most extraordinary measures could possibly hope to work? Roerich, as a humanitarian of profound occult gifts himself with an unswerving dedication to the aims of Shamballah may well have been deemed a suitable vehicle to receive this exceptional sign of favour and occult assistance. Can we, in fact, at least consider the possibility that the Nazis were responsible for the subsequent crop of flying-saucer sightings caused by their own contact with black-magic groups within Tibet? Certainly, both in Tibet and Germany, the black orders had thrown in their lot with Haushofer and Hitler. Was 'the sign of Shambhala' the response of the Masters themselves to the imminent threat to world civilization posed by the Nazis and their Satanic collaborators? This hypothesis has never before been considered; and yet it seems deeply relevant to the whole question of Nazi occult activities. We can, I think, at least entertain the idea that the whole phenomenon of flying saucers rests directly upon the decision of Haushofer to recruit unsavoury occult allies from among the black lodges of Tibet. If this theory is correct, we must be grateful to the Masters of Shamballah for taking action on behalf of the occult opposition to Nazism. On the other hand, we might question whether flying saucers are not an extreme case of a thought-form projected with such power that they took on a life of their own, continuing to appear long after the original situation which had provoked their manifestation had passed away for good.

11 Hitler as Conjuror

We have already seen that Hitler was born in 'medium country', and that he shared the same wet-nurse as Willi Schneider, the gifted psychic. We have traced how deeply Hitler delved into occult brotherhoods, seeking to grasp the hidden wisdom and turn it to his own destructive and selfish ends. His lifelong obsession with the Spear of Destiny has also been studied in some detail. It is now time for us to turn to the most basic questions of all. What actual psychic powers did Hitler possess? And how did he come by them?

The influence of such men as Haushofer and Eckart has already been chronicled. We have also seen the deep impact that certain philosophers, poets, musicians and occultists had upon him. Now we must turn to the constitution of his own peculiar psyche.

The two most obvious features of Hitler's occult character are his precognitive ability and his intense, not to say overpowering, personal magnetism. Hardly less important was his ability to interact with the unconscious emotions of a large crowd. With Hitler's precognitive abilities we shall deal in the next chapter. Let us begin by considering his personal magnetism.

Hitler came from an upper-working-/lower-middle-class background. In spite of this he was easily able to dominate men from a far higher social background than himself. Although he had been decorated for gallantry during the First World War, he had still only reached the rank of corporal. And yet even seasoned generals trembled before him. Even hard-bitten men like Röhm were willing to serve under a mere corporal. Such an exceptional ability to command loyalty sprang from his own intense charisma and ability to persuade people to his point of view. But it was no ordinary power of persuasion that Hitler had.

William Shirer, author of the monumental *The Rise and Fall of the Third Reich*, described his experience of a rally in 1934 at which Hitler appeared briefly. He noticed particularly the ecstasy in the faces of the women as they looked at the orator on the stage. They reminded Shirer of the Holy Rollers, a religious sect whose members leaped about and rolled all over the floor, sometimes for hours. They gazed on Hitler as if he were some kind of superhuman messiah, their faces contorted into an almost sexual ecstasy. If he had stayed on the platform much longer, Shirer felt, some of the women would have fainted from their inner excitement.[1]

During the early years of Nazi rule, there were many times when even Hitler's associates were convinced that what he wanted was unrealistic and could never be achieved. Even earlier, during the Nazis' rise to power, Hitler again and again managed to convince people who disliked him personally and who disagreed with his aims and objectives to give way or come over to his opinion.

The most notorious example of the power of his personal magnetism came in 1926. A conference was held at Bamberg to try and heal the split in the party between the socialist and conservative wings. There, a motion was put to the membership calling for the expropriation of the property of the former German royal family. Hitler opposed the resolution which Goebbels had proposed. The latter had actually called for 'the expulsion of the *petit-bourgeois* Adolf Hitler from the National Socialist Party' so radical were Goebbels's views in those days. Hitler delivered a powerful speech which produced the extraordinary result of Goebbels standing up and publicly saying that he had been mistaken and would from now on support Hitler. And this kind of thing occurred again and again.[2] Countless instances of people, by no means weak-willed themselves, who found their powers of judgement and resistance completely overcome by Hitler, are certain testimony to his extraordinary persuasiveness. In crowds, he could whip up a fever of mass hysteria; but even on the level of personal contact, it was almost impossible for people to withstand his powers of personal magnetism.

Men as powerful and charismatic as Goering, Goebbels, Schacht and von Blomberg were completely unable to withstand his spell. Admiral Dönitz, the commander-in-chief of the navy, actually said, 'I purposefully went very seldom to his headquarters, for I had the feeling that I would thus best preserve my powers of initiative, and also because, after several days at headquarters, I always had the feeling that I had to disengage myself from his powers of suggestion. I am telling you this because in this connection I was doubtless more fortunate than his staff, who were constantly exposed to his power and personality.'[3]

In 1943, when Mussolini had been deposed and the German army had rescued him from the new anti-Fascist government in Italy, Hitler brought him to Germany and deliberately infused Mussolini with some of his own power. 'By putting every ounce of nervous energy into the effort,' Hitler said, 'I succeeded in pushing Mussolini back on to the rails. In those four days the *Duce* underwent a complete change. When he got out of the train on his arrival he looked like a broken old man. When he left again he was in high fettle, ready for anything.' Thus we see how Hitler was able to use his own powers of personal magnetism to recharge, as it were, Mussolini's batteries.[4] So intense was this effect that even men like the minister of defence, von Blomberg, could say, 'I know you are right, but I have confidence in Hitler. He will find some solution.'[5] Even in the bunker at Berlin, with Russian troops only miles away, he still retained his powers of domination over men.

> Until the last days of his life [Alan Bullock wrote], he retained an uncanny gift of personal magnetism which defies analysis, but which many who met him have described. Hitler's powers to bewitch an audience has been likened to the occult arts of the African medicine-man or the Asiatic shaman; others have compared it to the sensitivity of a medium and the magnetism of a hypnotist.[6]

And Trevor-Roper wrote of 'the mysterious intensity of those dull, glaucous eyes, the messianic egotism of that harsh, oracular voice'.[7] Shirer, too, spoke of the 'magic words of the Austrian', under the spell of which the audience seemed to surrender their wills and emotions.[8]

An anti-Nazi Englishman once attended a rally at which Hitler spoke. He did not understand German, but under the influence of Hitler's mesmeric oratory he found his own emotions aroused, in spite of having understood nothing of the speech. To his astonishment he found himself giving the Nazi salute and shrieking 'Heil Hitler!' with the rest of the crowd.[9]

We know that during his youth Hitler read many books on hypnotism and studied the great orators throughout history. Kubizek, his boyhood friend, remarks that once, after seeing Wagner's *Rienzi*, Hitler told him excitedly that he too would one day be able to spellbind crowds with the power of oratory. In *Mein Kampf*, Hitler openly attached great powers to the art of oratory. 'The power which has always started the greatest religions and political avalanches in history rolling has from time immemorial been the magic power of the spoken word. The broad masses of the people can be moved only by the power of speech. All great movements and popular movements, volcanic eruptions of human passions and emotions, were stirred by the firebrand of the word hurled among the masses.'[10]

Hitler also stated that the process of overcoming opposition in a crowd cannot be achieved by rational arguments, but rather by an appeal to 'hidden forces'. As Otto Strasser put it,

> Hitler responds to the vibration of the human heart with the delicacy of a seismograph, or perhaps a radio-receiving set, enabling him, with a certainty with which no conscious gift could endow him, to act as a loudspeaker proclaiming the most secret desires, the least admissable instincts, the sufferings and personal revolts of a whole nation. Speaking as the spirit moves him, he is transformed into one of the greatest speakers of the century. Adolf Hitler enters a hall. He sniffs the air. For a minute he gropes, feels his way, senses the atmosphere. Suddenly he bursts forth. His words go like an arrow to their target, he touches each private wound on the raw, liberating the mass unconscious, expressing its innermost aspirations, telling it what it wants to hear.[11]

What was it, then, that gave Hitler this astonishing power over men and women? Was it a form of hypnotism, or the brilliance of his oratory, or mediumship, or shamanism? Or were there darker reasons for the spell Hitler cast upon the soul and destiny of a whole people?

Hypnotism might explain some of the extraordinary effect he had over individuals. But hypnotists work essentially by relaxing their subject and then directing their energy upon his or her lowered resistance to suggestion. Hitler does not appear to have done this. No one ever felt relaxed in the presence of the German leader. It is true that the nature and origin of hypnotic powers is still a much discussed subject; but that relaxation is an essential ingredient is agreed by all. Whatever powers Hitler may have been using, then, they were not hypnotic ones.

Nor does the hypothesis of mass hypnosis account for his power over crowds, because this requires the orator to produce collective hallucinations among large numbers of people. The most famous example is probably the Indian rope trick. An eyewitness of this phenomenon described to me how the hypnotist builds up a picture of what he wants his audience to see. He tells them in detail about the basket in which the rope is kept, and the rope itself; and then, at the right psychological moment, when he has built up the illusion sufficiently, he throws the rope up into the air. Even though it actually falls down again, because of the web of words which the fakir has woven about his audience, they see exactly what he has told them to see – the illusion of a straight rope hanging in the air, and a boy climbing up it. Hitler might have been able to convince people to believe and do things which they would not otherwise have done, but even he did not produce mass hallucinations in Germany or anywhere else. And, as with normal hypnosis, the key to the fakir's success is his ability to relax his audience. Hitler, as I have remarked, did the opposite.

Since it is quite clear, then, in spite of Hitler's known interest in hypnotism, that it is not the latter which offers the key to his powers, where should we look for an alternative explanation?

The Swiss occultist and physician Paracelsus believed that the essence of life resided in a substance called 'mummia'. This was an invisible substance, though it could be attracted by making a magnet from blood, urine, excrement, sweat and hair. All these substances contain the vital forces of the body from which they have come, and a magnet made from them would draw mummia to it. Paracelsus made extensive use of magnets generally, trying to extract the 'nervous fluid' from the body. We know that at least one Nazi leader took Paracelsus's ideas seriously, for Rudolf Hess used to sleep with magnets under his bed to draw off 'harmful emanations'.[12] It is possible that Hitler might have come across Paracelsus and his magnetic treatments through Hess, but considering the extent of Hitler's own occult activities, and his known interest in hypnotism and oratory even when he was living in a Vienna doss-house, it seems more likely that Hitler already knew about Paracelsus before he met Hess. Paracelsus, after all, is one of the great names of occultism, and it would be more surprising if Hitler was not familiar with him than if he was.[13]

However, even if Hitler had not studied the ideas of Paracelsus – which seems unlikely – there is another source which he would certainly have known. Two hundred years after Paracelsus, the Austrian doctor Franz Mesmer published a work which claimed that the movements of the planets directly affected the human body. This effect was produced through the action of an invisible fluid. Everything in the universe was supposed to be dipped in this fluid. At first Mesmer called it electricity, but later renamed it 'animal magnetism', since it had magnetic properties and seemed to act mainly on living beings. Mesmer thought that in the same way as a magnet has two poles, so man has two magnetic poles, those on his left being opposite to those on his right. In every human being there should be a proper balance of animal magnetism, and illness results from an imbalance. By restoring the polarity of the opposites, health can be restored. There are two ways of doing this: either by stroking the body with magnets or through the exercise of willpower. Mesmer believed that the magnetic fluid responded to a controlling will.[14]

After numerous experiments with magnets and sulphuric fluids, Mesmer came to the conclusion that physical magnetism was not involved in the process of animal magnetism. He decided that a universal fluid existed within the human body, and simply the touch of a hand could effect a cure.

Mesmer soon attracted disciples who, like himself, began to use Mesmerism as a curative for various medical ills. As he was succeeding where the orthodox doctors were failing, he drew strong hostility from the medical Mafia, who got together and pressurized him into leaving Vienna for Paris. For six years he was allowed to practise there, before the French doctors decided to produce a report which claimed that there was no such thing as animal magnetism, and that 'the excitement of the imagination' was responsible for the cures. 'From a curative point of view,' the Royal Society of Medicine decided, 'animal magnetism is nothing but the art of making sensitive people fall into convulsions.'

The curious thing is that, although most people for a long time have viewed Mesmerism as a form of hypnotism, the methods were completely different. To begin with, there was no relaxation; excitement and convulsions were the rule. No modern hypnotist can duplicate the effects which Mesmer achieved. Secondly, there is the marked similarity of symptoms between Mesmer's patients and many of Hitler's acquaintances. Thus the French Major du Hussey found 'ice came from my limbs, followed by great heat'. And visitors to Hitler, especially when he was in one of his notorious bouts of bad temper, described experiencing nervous sensations of extreme cold and heat. Thirdly, Mesmer only had to appear in a room for excitement to reach fever pitch among his patients; another parallel with the effects of Hitler's appearances in public.[15]

Finally, the Soviet Union discovered the techniques known as Kirlian photography. This has shown the reality of phenomena previously written off as superstitious occult nonsense, such as the aura and animal magnetism. The Soviet scientists succeeded in charting and measuring the exact flow of animal magnetism or, as they called it, bio-plasmic energy, in the human body. There is now little doubt that Mesmerism, or animal magnetism, is a real force in nature. What is more significant, Kirlian photography has shown that faith healers, psychokineticists, mediums and other occultists can use it to produce some of their most striking effects.[16]

Now there also seems little doubt that this animal magnetism, or bio-plasmic energy, is the same force as the Vril Society, to which Hitler and other top Nazis belonged, called by the name of *vril* power.[17] It also seems likely to be the same force which Oriental occultists call '*prana*'. Now both Hitler and Mesmer were Austrians; both were interested in the occult and astrology; both were astonishingly charismatic; both produced excitement and convulsions in their audiences. And Mesmer's animal magnetism is nothing other than the *vril* power used by the Nazi leader under a different name. There is also the curious fact that Mesmer believed that the magnetic fluid yielded to a controlling will. And Hitler said on many occasions that people and situations could be made to bend before a superior will. Enough evidence has been produced, I think, to convince all but the most dogmatic doubter that Hitler had discovered the force of Mesmerism, and used it to devastating effect to transform individuals and events.[18]

We come back once more to the extraordinary influence which his reading of *Parsifal* had upon Hitler. In this legend, mention is made of the power of the word which becomes the 'word-sword', and through which men may be moved for good or evil.[19] Hitler, as we know, used the power of words for evil effects. During his political career, Hitler made literally thousands of public speeches. At the beginning, he found giving them an exhausting and traumatic experience. But before long he found it an invigorating and revitalizing one.

Obviously the more speeches Hitler made the better he became at public speaking; but this does not explain how a speech could leave him feeling more vital than before. And there is no doubt that, as Hitler spoke, he did not lose power, but gained it. By the end of a speech he was almost in the same state as that of a trance medium, expressing the unconscious aspirations of the vast crowd. Such a mediumistic expression of oratory is even more tiring than ordinary public speaking; and yet Hitler seemed refreshed and reinvigorated by these events. In the words of his close friend and associate Albert Speer, 'he drew more impetus and courage from those mass meetings than he himself had poured out'.[20]

There is no rational explanation for this phenomenon; but there is an occult explanation which covers all the facts. Nothing but the superstitions of positivism prevent us from conceding that the occult explanation of Hitler makes sense, is consistent, and explains aspects of his career which are inexplicable on any other hypothesis. The occult account of Hitler's powers is quite clear. The Nazi leader was one of those individuals who feed off others' energy, who radiate enormous charges of personal magnetism but recharge their own batteries by drawing off the psychic life-forces of other people. Hitler, in short, was what is known among the fraternity of occultists as a 'psychic vampire'.[21] It is astonishing how, time and again, individuals coming into contact with Hitler complained that they felt exhausted after meeting him. Speer comments thus on Hitler and his colleagues: 'They were all under his spell, blindly obedient and with no will of their own – whatever the medical term for this phenomenon may be. I noticed during my activities as architect, that to be in his presence for any length of time made me tired, exhausted and void.'[22]

Now Speer, unlike most of Hitler's associates, was highly sceptical about occult beliefs; he did not actually suggest that Hitler was a psychic vampire. But only that particular explanation accounts for, not only Hitler's devitalizing effect on individuals, but also his ability to replenish his nervous energy by public speaking.

In this context it is highly significant that Hitler made very few public appearances after the beginning of the war. After 1942 he stopped almost completely, making only four speeches. And two of them were funeral orations for dead party members. The thing that everyone who was close to Hitler noticed was that he was beginning to get tired and run-down. Obviously the stress of managing the war effort, plus the ordinary effects of aging, must have played their part in this process. But his doctors said that Hitler showed signs of premature senility. He was also complaining of giddiness, stomach cramps and tremblings in his arms and legs. All the doctors who examined Hitler during the war came to the conclusion that these things were the result of a psychosomatic disorder. Indeed, if Hitler was a psychic vampire who was no longer able to 'feed', that is exactly what we would expect to happen. Especially since Hitler still went on exercising his own extraordinary powers of personal magnetism.[23]

Why, since Hitler must have known that the only way to recharge his batteries was via oratory, did he almost stop his personal appearances? Hitler told his doctors that he was too tired to appear in public any more, and his generals were informed that he was too busy with the war effort. But the real reason was the one he told Goebbels: that he could not face a German crowd until he had a major victory to report to it. For by 1942 it was clear that the Germans were slowly losing the war. Because of this, Hitler dared not face the crowds again. Had he done so, the focus of their resentment and hatred would have switched away from the Jews, Communists and the Treaty of Versailles, and over to him. Only if another battle could be won could Hitler appear before his people and again be the mouthpiece of Germany's glory. Till then, all he could do was make the occasional prepared speech to select gatherings of loyal party members.[24]

Another reason why Hitler began to lose his touch badly after 1942 is connected with an occult technique of attaining intuitive consciousness by deliberately overbreathing (hyperventilation). This he was particularly prone to do at his large public appearances. Once he stopped making speeches, he lost his ability to become a trance medium. After this, his intuition failed him, and he was reduced, more or less, to guesswork.[25]

We have already dealt in some detail with the nature and extent of Hitler's involvement in black magic and Satanic rituals. We have also studied his astrological activities, his use of Mesmerism and his psychic vampirism. The grail legends and the Spear of Destiny were also decisive influences on Hitler's fate. And now again the legendary figure of Klingsor, the man of whom Hitler believed himself to be a reincarnation, comes into our story once more.

Both Hitler and Stein believed that the Klingsor of *Parsifal* was Landulf of Capua. And, of course, Landulf, like Hitler, used the reversed swastika as his heraldic device. But there was another Klingsor to enter the grail legends, this time in 1207. He was a bishop who won a contest of poetry and song among the Minnesingers. This Klingsor was supposed to have been a master of black magic and to have sold himself to the Devil in return for his bishopric. According to the legend, he had escaped into Hungary and became the secret founder of the Inquisition. At the same time arose the legend of the Pied Piper of Hamelin, who was able to lure the town's children to follow him by playing his flute, and they went after him into a cave hidden in the hills. This legend, so occultists have discovered, refers to the way in which a black magician can infect the souls of a whole people. Hitler, in this way, corrupted the souls of the German nation.[26]

Among his other occult obsessions, Hitler believed that he was a reincarnation of this Bishop Klingsor. Furthermore he claimed that in yet another incarnation he had been the notoriously cruel and depraved Roman Emperor Tiberius. In 1937 he sent Goering to San Michele, where the tyrant spent the last few years of his reign, to try to buy the island from the Swedish writer Axel Munthe. Unfortunately, Munthe also believed himself to be the reincarnation of Tiberius, so refused to sell his island, in spite of the fabulous sum Goering offered him. Goering, along with Goebbels, claimed that in every one of Hitler's previous incarnations, he too had been reborn along with this Führer.[27]

The idea of Hitler as a kind of Satanic Pied Piper, a black magician who seduced the souls of a whole people, seems to fit the character and destiny of the German leader perfectly. That Hitler had more than average, perhaps more than merely human, abilities is without doubt. Equally certain is the fact that he directed those powers wholly towards destructive ends. In the pursuit of power and demonic mastery over nations and men, millions of lives were sacrificed needlessly to the greater glory of Adolf Hitler and his Satanic vision. Between the powers that Hitler served and those of his enemies, white magicians like Stein and Steiner, there could be no compromise. When the Nazis unleashed war upon the whole world, forces that not even their opponents were aware of came to their aid against the massed assault of Hitler and his Satanic cohorts. Hitler was a magician, a conjurer, of more than ordinary power. Under his spell, a great country dragged itself down to destruction, taking many millions of lives with it in the death-throes of its inevitable defeat. As the Pied Piper had driven the rats into the river, so Hitler drove people into the darkness of death and destruction.

12 Seeing into the Future

Time is one of the great mysteries of the human race. In our conventional concept of time, precognition – the ability to see into the future – is impossible, since the future has not yet taken place. And yet there is abundant evidence that precognition does take place, more than almost any other aspect of the occult. But how, on the standard model of time as a kind of ladder stretching from past into future, can this be?

The only answer that conventional thinkers can offer is the unrewarding blind alley of determinism, which claims that every single event that has ever occurred or ever will occur was preordained at the beginning of time. Apart from the difficulties of reconciling this view with our actual experience of ourselves as having free will, it poses the further question: Who or what is doing the determining? And why? As such, whatever its pretensions to be a scientific hypothesis, it is essentially a superstitious way of pretending to know what we do not know. Determinism is the pseudo-scientific equivalent of those philosophical theories that start with an incredible position, realize its difficulties and then drag in God to dig them out of the mess. Determinism is a deistic theory for people who cannot bear to admit the existence of randomness and chance in the universe. It is, quite simply, ignorance pretending to be knowledge.

As Kant demonstrated conclusively 200 years ago, to any unbiased intellect, space and time do not have real, independent existence as absolute entities. They are, rather, structures of our minds, or, to put it more simply, without the concepts of space and time we would be unable to make sense of the world as we actually experience it. We do not experience space and time; what we experience are events which we are forced, in order for our minds to be able to organize the data we receive through our senses, to perceive as events related to us by the forms of space and time.[1] As Einstein showed conclusively, what we experience is not time, but a process of duration. We know the relative motion of objects as they appear to us, and abstract this motion and call it space and time. But because we do experience everything under the forms of space and time, we fall into the error of thinking that they have real existence, instead of being concepts which our mind requires in order to function in the world of experience. This fundamental error, often referred to by philosophers as 'naive realism', is at the heart of the determinist fallacy.

If we adopt the model of time offered by Einstein and Kant, we can see how it is possible for us to see into the future. For there is no real future, past or present, only our minds and their relation to objects at any given 'point-instant'. The future, then, is not what has not yet happened, for the whole idea of such a linear time is an incoherent hypothesis. There are only events, not fixed in time, which we perceive through our unconscious mind and later appear to us in reality under the form of the future.

Precognitive ability is linked to psychic senses generally. As we have already seen, Hitler was abundantly gifted with magical and occult powers. And many of his actions make sense only on the assumption that he was a precognitive. They make no sense at all on any other hypothesis, unless we are prepared to stretch coincidence to points which are more incredible than the alternative account, the precognitive one. The orthodox account also has the unfortunate consequence of requiring us to reject the unequivocal testimony of hundreds of eyewitnesses who did claim that precognition was a major factor in Hitler's career.[2]

The reality of precognition has now been demonstrated to such an extent that only blind dogmatism can account for the continuing refusal of a minority to accept it as a simple fact of our experience. No one appears to have achieved a success rate of 100 per cent; but eighty per cent has been achieved even under the most strictly controlled laboratory conditions. One wonders how Hitler would have performed in such a test situation. For there is no doubt at all that he possessed above-average precognitive powers.

To begin with, there is Hitler's own account of how he came to join the Nazi Party or, as it was then called, the German Workers Party. Hitler went along to a party meeting on the instructions of his superiors, was bored by what he heard and then angry at it. The Party's treasury was almost bare, its membership laughably small. Nor did any of the men he encountered at the meeting inspire him with any enthusiasm at all. He returned home again, totally disillusioned with the Party and convinced that it could never become a major force in German and world history.

Two days later, Hitler was seized by a sudden sense of historic destiny. He knew that somehow he could take this tiny band and transform it into an instrument to restore the greatness of Germany. On any rational assessment, Hitler would have done just as well to have forgotten about Drexler and his movement, go somewhere else and try again. There were other larger German nationalist groupings available to him. He could even have gone off and founded his own party, where he alone would have dictated policy and chosen his own inner council. Yet Hitler decided to throw his weight behind the tiny German Workers Party. He had no reason to do so at all; yet an unyielding inner sense told him that he should do so. As everyone knows, his decision was doubtless the 'right' one; yet it was equally certainly not the rational one. But, of course, Hitler's own inner sense, his precognitive insight, told him that his decision to join was the correct thing to do.[3]

Before long, of course, Hitler met Eckart, and a few years later, Haushofer. They must have considerably increased and developed Hitler's own natural psychic abilities. As time passed his own powers of foresight must have grown enormously. And with his eventual rise to the leadership of Germany he was at last able to use them to their fullest extent.

Hitler came to power in 1933 as the head of a coalition government in which his own party was a minority partner. He could have been dismissed at any minute by the German president. Most men, in these circumstances, would have been cautious and tentative in their political approach. Not Hitler, though. Hardly had he been appointed chancellor than he began a secret – and completely illegal – programme of German military rearmament.

All Hitler's political and military advisers thought that he was making a terrible mistake, and said so. Even the German generals did not believe that the Allies would allow the Germans to go on rearming in defiance of the Treaty of Versailles. Yet Hitler took no notice of them. There was no risk of war, he insisted. The Allies would do nothing about it. To the economists who argued that Germany could not afford to pay for the cost of a strengthened military establishment, Hitler was equally firm. Rearmament will not weaken the economy, he told them. In fact, it will strengthen it.[4]

This belief of Hitler's was absolute heresy within the accepted economic ideas of that time. All the German economists threw up their hands in despair and decided that Hitler was mad. But, despite unanimous opposition by the money men, Hitler took no notice. He appointed his own minister of economics and ordered him to carry out the policies he wanted. He also pressed ahead relentlessly with his rearmament programme. The result, all the experts said, would be disaster. In fact, as Hitler had predicted, it had exactly the opposite effect. The level of German unemployment fell steadily at first, and before long dramatically. Hitler was right, and the experts had been wrong – but not because he had studied any new economic theories which made him realize that his predecessors had got it wrong. In fact, if there was one subject that really bored Hitler, it was economics. But he did not listen to any experts who provided an alternative strategy; rather, he heeded the promptings of his inner voice. Hitler just *knew* that he was right. Once again, his precognition proved more correct than the 'rational' judgements of the orthodox economists.[5]

By 1935 it was known to all and sundry that the Germans had broken the Treaty of Versailles and were secretly rearming. The British government published a White Paper which expressed particular concern about the development of a completely illegal air force. The German generals, faced with an open condemnation of the secret rearmament policy, expressed grave disquiet to Hitler. But the chancellor brushed their objections aside. The British will do nothing, he told them. In fact, since you are so worried about our secret rearmament policy, I will make it easier for you. We will end the farce for good.[6]

This paraphrase of what Hitler told his military advisers led to his boldest step so far. He publicly renounced the military sections of the Versailles Treaty and began to rearm openly. He also introduced conscription, another thing which the Versailles Treaty had forbidden the Germans to do.

Secret rearmament was bad enough, but open defiance of the Allies in such a sensitive area was quite another. There was no telling how they would react. If they had gone to war, with Germany at the time, on the clear-cut issue of that country's breaking a treaty which she herself had signed, there is no question that the Germans would have been quickly defeated. The French government, which at the time had the strongest army in Europe, virtually begged Britain to join them in a preventative war. But the British government hesitated, blustered and finally did nothing. Reluctant to go it alone, the French too backed down. Hitler's astonishing gamble had paid off. Against all the advice of his generals, against all reasonable expectation of how the Allies would behave, Hitler had taken a calculated risk and got away with it. Just as he had predicted, the Allies did nothing.[7]

Next year Hitler rubbed salt into the wound, violating the Treaty of Locarno (of which Germany was also a co-signatory) by sending German troops into the Rhineland. Under the provisions of the Locarno Treaty this area had been specifically laid down as a demilitarized zone. Again the German generals begged Hitler not to push his luck. This time, they argued, the French might not be so willing to let the Germans get away with it. After all, the Rhineland backed directly on to French soil. But Hitler rejected their arguments contemptuously. You have no need to be afraid, he told them. Last year the French threatened war but they backed down. They will do nothing. And, in spite of all the odds being stacked against him, Hitler was right. He *knew* that not a shot would be fired in anger. Nor was it. The French appealed instead to the League of Nations.[8]

Two years later Hitler sent German troops into Austria to forcibly incorporate it into the German Reich. Once more the generals advised Hitler against it. This time, the Allies were incensed by Hitler's actions. His foreign minister, Ribbentrop, was in London at the time and had to lie through his teeth to calm the tempers of the British government. The reports were only mistaken rumours, he told them. Of course German troops have not moved into Austria. But, of course, they had. And, in spite of the fury they felt at this latest act of Nazi aggression, in spite of the intense alarm that both Ribbentrop and the German generals felt at the prospect of an imminent war with Britain and France, Hitler was confident that nothing would be done about the Austrian annexation. He *knew* that there would be no war over Austria. And he was right, again in disregard of the opinions of his military advisers.[9]

Later that year he began to harass the government of Czechoslovakia, using the excuse of persecution of the German population in the Sudetenland. By September of that year the situation was so bad that Shirer, who was in Prague at the time, wrote in his diary, 'War is very near.' Once more Hitler's military advisers urged caution upon him; yet again he took no notice of them. And once again, he turned out to be right. Even Chamberlain's visit to Munich led to no softening in Hitler's attitude. In fact, he simply increased his demands. Not until the second visit to Munich by Chamberlain did Hitler at last agree to a settlement. And the settlement to which the Allies agreed amounted to unconditional surrender on their part. Considering the sabre-rattling they had been indulging in at the beginning of the Czechoslovakian crisis, it was an astonishing capitulation to Hitler's demands. Once again, Hitler had been proved right and his advisers wrong. Yet again, his precognitive gifts had not failed him. France and Britain will do nothing, his voices told him; and France and Britain did indeed do nothing. Yet again he had taken a bold, even reckless gamble, which by all reasonable lights should have ended in war, and got away with it.[10]

The following year German troops, in direct violation of the Munich agreement which Hitler had only just signed, marched into Czechoslovakia and occupied it. The anger which Britain in particular felt at this latest act of aggression was such that overnight Winston Churchill changed from being one of the least to one of the most popular men in Britain. Chamberlain had all his illusions about Hitler cruelly destroyed in a single day, and he was furious. As for Churchill, he was now being widely tipped for the leadership of the Conservative Party, now that Chamberlain's appeasement policy had been such an abject failure. There was, yet again, a real danger of war; but, once more, the Allies did not bring the matter to a head. Once more Hitler's precognitive powers had not failed him.[11]

Even when, in September 1939, in response to the German invasion of Poland, Britain and France finally did declare war, it was, at first, in name only. Instead there followed the long period of military inactivity which became known as the Phoney War. So, even though at first glance it might look as if Hitler's precognitive powers had failed him in September 1939 – since Britain and France did declare war – as they did not actually fire a shot in anger, it seems that Hitler was right about that too. For Hitler had asked himself what Britain and France would do if he invaded Poland, and the answer he had received was that they would do nothing. And, of course, they did do absolutely nothing, just as Hitler's precognitive powers had told him. Once more his occult vision had been correct when all the rational evidence pointed the other way.[12]

In 1940 Hitler launched his western offensive, which again provoked his generals' dissent. The French and British armies were too strong, they argued. It was one thing beating the Poles, but you cannot expect to defeat the French so soon. It would be better just to sit tight and wait for the Allies to come to their senses. If we just do nothing, in time they will make peace.

Hitler brushed all their arguments contemptuously aside. Prepare for war, he told his generals. It will be a short campaign. Soon we will be in Paris. The generals heard his words, but they were filled with misgivings. They simply did not believe that the Germans could defeat the French army as easily as the Poles had been overrun. And yet, once again, Hitler was right and the rational arguments of his military strategists were wrong.[13]

It was in Poland that Hitler made one of his most puzzling speeches, on 19 September 1939. Poland had been completely defeated. Though in Warsaw there was still some sporadic resistance, for all practical purposes, the war was over. Hitler was in Danzig as a conquering hero.

The dictator strode masterfully on the rostrum of the city hall. At first he was full of praise for the German victories. But suddenly, in the middle of his speech, his face grew dark with anger, as he spoke of Britain. Screaming in a paroxysm of fury against the British, he swore, 'We will never capitulate.'

What sense did it make, with Germany in the driving-seat, to talk of capitulation? If anybody was going to surrender, the Allies looked more vulnerable than the Germans. What sense could capitulation have made when Germany was on top? The only explanation is that Hitler had suddenly been seized with a precognitive vision of his ultimate defeat as a result of British intransigence and refusal to make peace with him or to surrender to the German arms which were everywhere victorious. After years of stunning, uninterrupted triumph against the odds, he was struck with the sudden realization that it had all been in vain, and that in spite of all his efforts, magical and otherwise, Germany was doomed to be defeated.[14]

How was it that Hitler managed to acquire his powers of precognition? He may, of course, have been born with them. This is quite probable, especially since he shared the same wet-nurse as the medium Willi Schneider. But there is no doubt that they developed dramatically after his involvement with Eckart and Haushofer. What techniques did they teach him?

We know that they taught him to use drugs to heighten his consciousness, and also the magical power of human sacrifice. But to judge from accounts of Hitler in some of his more demented states, they also taught him a system of yoga breath-control. Hitler was nicknamed the '*Teppischfresser*', or 'carpet-eater': he used to foam at the mouth and roll around on the floor, chewing the carpet frantically. Rauschning gives an account of Hitler in a trance state, which strongly suggests that Hitler used just such a technique of overbreathing. 'He wakes up in the night, screaming and in convulsions. He appears to be half paralysed. He utters confused and unintelligible sounds, gasping as if on the point of suffocation.'

Deliberate overbreathing increases the flow of oxygen to the brain and produces trance-like states. This kind of account by Rauschning strongly suggests that Hitler, desperate for further prophetic insights, often overdid the process and succumbed to oxygen 'drunkenness'.[15]

Why is it, though, that Hitler's precognitive powers seem abruptly to have deserted him after 1942? Obviously it could be argued that Hitler had never been more than lucky at guessing, and the prophetic dice no longer rolled in his favour. But this explanation does not cover all the facts. What seems more likely is that Hitler used his overbreathing technique chiefly during the height of his frenzy when speaking in public. Since he stopped making them after 1942, he never again reached the same degree of trance and thus could not get his intuitive powers to function properly.[16]

Another reason why Hitler's visionary powers started to forsake him is almost certainly connected to his drug-taking activities.[17] Psychedelic drugs have the effect of destroying or weakening the power of serotonin to hold the mind together. Serotonin is manufactured in the pineal gland, which occultists call the third eye and the French philosopher Descartes regarded as the seat of the soul in man. Schizophrenics always have less serotonin in the brain than ordinary people. What seems likely is that, as a result of his drug-abuse, Hitler succeeded in suppressing the inhibitory functions of the rational part of the mind, the left-hand side of his brain. As a result he was no longer able to control the vagaries of his unconscious, the source of his precognitive powers.[18]

On any unbiased reading of the facts, then, Hitler indeed possessed powers of prophecy well above the average. These were partly natural gifts, partly acquired through the use of psychedelic drugs and various magical practices. And, after years of abusing his body and corrupting his moral sense, they simply went away for good. Not once after 1942 was Hitler able to make a successful prediction; yet up to then he had made dozens of them. As was once truly said, 'Whom the gods would destroy, they first make mad.'

13 Nostradamus Speaks

In the previous chapter we studied Hitler's astonishing ability to see into the future. But the most famous, and remarkable, of all prophets and foretellers is unquestionably the French occultist Nostradamus.

In a small French town, Salon de Croix, in the year 1550, Nostradamus performed a magical ritual, at the end of which he fell into a trance and his body shook with convulsions – remarkably similar symptoms to some of those Hitler was to demonstrate. After he came round, Nostradamus wrote down a poem of only four lines, which he claimed had been dictated to him by a spirit. There followed, over the next few years, a thousand prophecies in verse.

Nostradamus studied astrology and medicine, becoming a gifted healer and skilled astrologer. But it was the impact of his astonishingly convoluted but often stunningly accurate account of events often two or three centuries later which guaranteed his immortality. Not surprisingly, both sides in the Second World War eagerly scanned the prophecies of Nostradamus in the hope of finding verses predicting victory for themselves.

One of the most astonishing of Nostradamus's quatrains, which can only refer to an event during the Second World War, is the following:

> The assembly will go out from the castle of Franco,
> The ambassador not satisfied will make a schism;
> Those of the Riviera will be involved,
> And they will deny the entry to the great gulf.[1]

In the first place, this is the only mention of Franco in the whole of Nostradamus. And, as we know, General Franco of Spain had declared his country 'non-belligerent on the Axis side' at the start of the war. In 1941 Franco met the Axis powers – *on the Riviera*. Hitler and Mussolini asked Franco for permission to allow German and Italian troops to pass through Spain into *the entry to the great gulf* – Gibraltar – which would have given the Axis powers control of the Mediterranean. Much to their astonishment and anger, Franco flatly refused to allow Axis troops to pass through Spain, even though it would have meant the annexation of Gibraltar to his country. At the time Hitler had not even attacked Russia, and German arms had been invincible everywhere. But Franco stood firm.

The odds against the name Franco, a meeting of ambassadors on the Riviera, and the denial of 'the entry to the great gulf' all occurring together by chance are more than one in a million. And this prophecy originates from the 1550s!

Another section of Nostradamus's prophecies which have been taken as referring to the war are the three 'Hister Quatrains'. It is claimed that Hister is meant to represent Hitler. Unfortunately the three verses in question are not only exceptionally obscure; it is also by no means certain that they do refer to Hitler, by implication or otherwise (though Nostradamus is renowned for hiding clues within puns and anagrams). The first of the three is the likeliest fit:

> Liberty will not be recovered.
> A bold, black, base-born, iniquitous man will occupy it;
> When the material of the bridge is completed,
> The republic of Venice will be annoyed by Hister.[2]

To begin with, this is appallingly obscure. More seriously, however, Hister is an old name for the River Danube. Thus it could refer to Hungary, Austria, Germany or even other countries. It is true that verbal conundrums were popular during the time of Nostradamus; but 'the republic of Venice' ceased to exist during the Napoleonic Wars. Trying to use it as a coded phrase for Italy under Mussolini seems to me to be stretching credibility. Far more likely is that the verses refer to Napoleon, who conquered Venice fresh from a campaign on the Danube. Hitler was certainly 'base-born'; but so was Napoleon. But there is a slight doubt as to the question of the bridge, which must refer in this context to one spanning the Danube. And, in 1941, the Nazis did build a bridge across that river. And within a month of its completion, the Germans began sending troops into Italy. This is strikingly similar to Nostradamus's prophecy; but the text is too obscure to judge properly. It may apply to Hitler, or to Napoleon. We cannot be certain here.

The second quatrain is, if possible, even more obscure than the last one:

> In place quite near, but far from Venus,
> The two greatest of Asia, and Africa
> It will be said that they are from the Rhine and Hister,
> Cries, tears at Malta, and Ligurian coast.[3]

Nostradamus always uses 'Venus' as a synonym for Venice. Again, then, there is an Italian connection. But who were the 'two greatest of Asia, and Africa'? Africa is relatively easy to make fit; they could have been Rommel and Montgomery. But 'the two greatest of Asia'? There were no Chinese or Japanese troops involved in the North African campaign. Nor did either Montgomery or Rommel serve in Asia. Mention of the Rhine and Hister certainly suggests a German connection, or perhaps an Austrian one. And there were 'tears at Malta, and Ligurian coast'. But quite what Nostradamus is getting at is altogether unclear. The only hint is the mention of Venice, which strongly implies a time no later than the Napoleonic Wars. So, once again, the attempt to make the Hister reference fit Hitler is inconclusive. The Maltese suffered appallingly at the hands of the Italians, and they successfully defended their island at the cost of many Italian lives. But the prophecy as a whole simply does not hang together. It could refer to almost anything.

The third and final Hister quatrain is as follows:

> Animals ferocious with hunger to swim rivers;
> Greater part of the camp will be against Hister,
> It will have the great man carried in an iron cage,
> When the German child watches the Rhine.[4]

Certainly, by the end of the Second World War, Germany, along with the countries it had occupied, was suffering acute hunger. It is also true that the 'greater part of the camp' were against Hitler by that time. But is it likely that Nostradamus is referring to the same person – if he is speaking of an individual at all – when he speaks of 'the great man', as he whom he has earlier called 'a bold, black, base-born, iniquitous man'? But the lines about 'when the German child watches the Rhine' ring true, and do suggest Hitler. With the Russians at the very gates of Berlin, German teenagers and even younger boys were put into uniform, given guns and ordered to protect the Fatherland as best they could. But, if Hitler was 'the great man' Nostradamus mentions, he was certainly not 'carried in an iron cage'. All in all, then, in spite of some interesting hits, and some still more puzzling obscurities, it cannot be argued with any degree of certainty that the Hister quatrains of Nostradamus do indeed refer to Adolf Hitler.

However, there are other verses in Nostradamus which do, with reasonable certainty, appear to refer to events during the Second World War. We have already seen the striking appropriateness of the Franco quatrain. Let us now turn our attention to more of Nostradamus's prophecies regarding World War II.

Those in the Isles a long time besieged
Will take vigour and strength against their enemies:
Those outside, dead with hunger, overthrown,
They will never be placed in a hunger to compare with it.[5]

When Nostradamus speaks of 'the Isles', he always means the British Isles. And in 1940, with the fall of France, it looked as if the Isles were doomed: they were indeed a 'long time besieged' during the Battle of Britain and under the German bombing raids, to say nothing of the sudden cessation of imports from Europe. But in the occupied countries of Europe – except for Spain, Portugal, Switzerland and Sweden – the people were indeed overthrown, and 'placed in a hunger' that they have not known since and had not known before for many a long year. The quatrain seems both clear and strikingly appropriate to the solitary resistance of Britain after the subjection of Europe under the Nazi yoke. Here, I feel, Nostradamus does make us feel that only the Battle of Britain can fit.

The next prophecy is also startling:

The Italian land will tremble near the mountains,
England and France will not be too well confederated.
They will help each other because of fear,
Only Castulon and the French will be curbed.[6]

This can only refer to a time after 1861, for until then Italy simply did not exist as a country. But, although Britain and France were actively hostile towards one another until 1904, after that date the *Entente Cordiale* was signed. From then on until the early 1920s, when Britain began to feel that France was becoming too harsh towards the Germans, they were close allies. Throughout the 1930s the French felt continually let down by the British. Far from helping each other, until the Nazi invasion of Poland they only stood together once against aggression. The first time was in 1934, when Hitler tried to stage a coup in Austria, and then in 1939, when he invaded Poland. Thus, in the entire course of human history since Nostradamus wrote this prophecy, there are only two possible dates which fit all the verses.

In 1934 Hitler instructed Nazi sympathizers within Austria to murder the chancellor and stage an uprising. But the result of the Austrian chancellor's assassination was to plunge Mussolini into a fury bordering on apoplexy. He at once gave orders for his troops to be mobilized along the Austrian border with Italy, and persuaded a reluctant Britain and France to form what was known as the Stresa Front against Nazi aggression. People tend to forget that until the Italians invaded Ethiopia in 1936, Mussolini was violently anti-Nazi. Any comparisons between his own Italian Fascism and German Nazism were indignantly repudiated by him. So, 'the Italian land' certainly trembled 'near the mountains' with the violence of Mussolini's reaction. Britain and France were anything but 'well confederated' in 1934, the French regarding the British as far too sympathetic to the Nazis. Still, at Mussolini's prompting, they did 'help each other because of fear' of renewed German aggression. But in what sense 'Castulon and the French' were 'curbed' by this entirely successful action – the last time the Allies stood up to Hitler before his invasion of Poland, and the only time in his political career he backed down – is unclear. Everything else fits the prophecy, except for the conclusion.

However, in 1938 Hitler sent his troops into Austria, and this time he did occupy it. By now Mussolini had become a German ally. All the same, the Italian land did tremble near the mountains, when the Germans marched into Austria. England and France were still not too well confederated; indeed, later that year they signed the Munich Agreement in an abject betrayal of the Czechoslovakian people. Fear of Hitler led them to try and buy him off by throwing the Czechs upon his tender mercies. In a sense, then, the French were curbed because of their fear of war; they therefore took no action when German troops marched illegally into Austria. But in 1939 Britain and France signed an alliance for mutual protection. The following year Germany had defeated France and the alliance was at an end, the French being truly 'curbed'.

The old Republican slogan of 'liberty, equality and fraternity' was banned by the Germans. Now in Latin 'castula' means a tunic; and the French figure of Liberty – equivalent in France to the figure of Britannia – wears a Roman tunic. Was Nostradamus saying in effect, 'Liberty and the French will be curbed'? If so, it makes sense of an otherwise baffling last line; and, like the 1934 events, it fits the facts of the quatrain adequately.

Here is the next relevant prophecy:

> The machines of flying fire
> Will come to worry the great commander of the besieged:
> Inside there will be such sedition,
> That the overthrown will be in despair.[7]

This could be a reference to aeroplanes; but a more likely explanation is that he is alluding to the flame-throwers which the Germans used against Belgium during their invasion of that country. These were flame-throwing tanks, operated by soldiers dressed in asbestos, which squirted blazing petrol and which produced tremendous confusion and alarm among the Belgian population. After their conquest of Belgium, the Germans used the same tactics against France. There is no doubt, moreover, that there was plenty of sedition within France in 1940. Indeed, another verse of Nostradamus refers to the establishment of the Vichy regime.

> An old man with the title of chief will arise, of doddering sense,
> Degenerating in knowledge and arms;
> Head of France (feared by his sister),
> The country divided, conceded to gendarmes.[8]

In the first place, Nostradamus speaks of the old man as 'Head of France', not king. There were no *gendarmes* in the sixteenth century, either. Pétain was eighty-four years old when he became leader of the Vichy regime, and considered by everyone to be 'of doddering sense'. After the German victory, France was divided into an occupied zone, under direct German control, and an unoccupied one, ruled by Pétain from Vichy. Pétain had been one of the great French heroes of the First World War, and had certainly once been a fine soldier. Hence the appropriateness of 'degenerating in knowledge and arms'. Moreover, at the time of his coming to power in 1940, Pétain had a sister-in-law still living, who, in an interview in *Time* magazine in July 1940, expressed her fears for France and said that her brother-in-law should not be head of France, because he was much too old. Every line in this prophecy is a palpable hit, and can only refer to Pétain and the establishment of Vichy rule.

Another amazing prophecy of Nostradamus refers to the failure of the much vaunted Maginot Line to protect France from the invading Germans. Even more incredibly, *two years before* the war had started a French scholar pointed out that Nostradamus was referring to the Maginot Line, even giving the correct number of sections into which it was divided.

> Near the great river, great retrenchment, earth withdrawn,
> It will be divided by the water into fifteen sections;
> The city will be taken, fire, blood, cries, all turmoil,
> And the greater part of the people confused by the shock.[9]

In Nostradamus's writings, 'the city' always means Paris. 'The great river' is, of course, the Rhine. The first line describes the building of trenches, the second the exact number of sections within the Maginot Line. The third predicts the fall of Paris, amid a welter of blood and turmoil; and the French people were certainly 'confused by the shock'. For years they had been told that the Maginot Line was impregnable; yet the Germans simply marched into France and took it over. Once again, each line of the four is on target, and can only refer to one event in French history.

The two remaining references in Nostradamus to events of the Second World War are, if anything, even more amazing. In the first one, he predicts the Battle of Britain; and in the second, the submarine blockade of Britain. The verses in question go:

> Because of the Germans, they and their neighbours around them
> Will be in wars for control of the clouds.[10]

It is impossible for this to refer to any event other than the Battle of Britain. In the first place, Germany did not even exist as a country until 1866, so how could they be at war before their existence? Secondly, 'wars for control of the clouds' can only refer to aerial combat. The only time the Germans fought 'for control of the clouds' were in the two world wars. It is, of course, possible that the verse refers instead to the dog-fights of the First World War; but, since air power was not a decisive factor in the First World War, while it undoubtedly was in the Second, it seems more likely altogether that Nostradamus is referring to the Battle of Britain. Especially when he also says: 'The armies will fight in the sky for a long time.'

The other, and final astonishing prophecy concerns what can only be the submarine. In the context referred to by Nostradamus, furthermore, it can only allude to an attempted submarine blockade.

> From where he thought to cause famine to come,
> From there will come abundance of supplies.
> The eye of the sea watches like a greedy dog,
> While one gives the other oil, wheat.[11]

Hitler hoped that by his use of submarine warfare he could prevent food from reaching Britain and starve her out. 'The eye of the sea' is surely the periscope of a submarine. And, thanks to the generous American Lend-Lease programme of Roosevelt, Britain did indeed receive 'abundance of supplies' from the United States.

Not surprisingly, Nostradamus's poetic oracles were of great interest to occultists on both sides during the war. It seems to have been Goebbels's wife who first thought of the idea of using them as occult propaganda. She read a quatrain which predicted that England would change her ruling family seven times within 290 years, and that there would be an international crisis involving France, Britain, Germany and Poland. As we know, this indeed came to pass. Predictably, Goebbels himself was impressed. He saw at once the possibilities of war of occult propaganda. However, in spite of his strenuous attempts to recruit German occultists to discover predictions by Nostradamus which foreshadowed a German victory, he was unable to find any. Not in the least discouraged, Goebbels found a simple way out of the problem: if no genuine prophecies could be found, he would simply have them forged.[12]

Krafft, whom we have come across already in the context of occult Nazi activities, was made responsible for fabricating the prophecies, and German aircraft subsequently dropped them over the French lines. Curiously enough, it was one of the more successful Nazi exercises in occult propaganda. The leaflets helped to inculcate an air of defeatism in the French people and their leaders. Indeed, so successful were they at achieving their purpose that the British became anxious.

Captain Louis de Wohl, Churchill's own personal astrologer, was thoroughly alarmed at the psychological success of the forged Nostradamus prophecies. He had some personal knowledge of Krafft and became attached to British Intelligence. Under his influence, the British government issued a German version of Nostradamus, which included no less than fifty 'prophecies' forged by de Wohl and his associates. It also contained a commentary which was full of anti-Nazi propaganda cleverly disguised as occult learning.[13]

Flushed with the success of his 'prophecies' in France, Krafft issued a whole book full of forged predictions and deliberate distortions of genuine Nostradamus quatrains to 'prove' that Britain was doomed to defeat at German hands. British Intelligence responded in kind, de Wohl and his colleagues coming up with more 'predictions' of Allied success.

In spite of the fact that the British did resort to the deliberate forging of Nostradamus prophecies for counter-intelligence reasons, there is little doubt that none of the verses in the genuine works could possibly be regarded as giving any support to the possibility of a German victory. Quite the reverse, in fact. Some examples of quatrains which could refer to Hitler are quite unflattering:

> The country will have made a bad choice.
> It will be heavier than its strength will enable it to endure.
> So great fury and rage will make men say
> That he will exterminate mankind by fire and sword.[14]

This quatrain is certainly an appropriate description of Hitler's rule. He was a bad choice for Germany, leading them to defeat and devastation in a bloody war. His most obvious characteristic was a choking hate, and at the end of the war, when even he could see that he had failed, his only answer was more terror. 'The German people have failed me,' he cried; 'they are not worthy of me!' Therefore, he decreed, the whole country of Germany, and its entire population, should be wiped out. 'World mastery or downfall' was, after all, the Nazi slogan. He actually succeeded in getting some of this insane policy executed; thus, for instance, 300,000 Germans were deliberately murdered when he ordered the flooding of the Berlin underground. Fortunately for the nation, Speer did his best to prevent Hitler's scorched-earth policy from being implemented.

Another judgement of Nostradamus on Hitler is this:

> An Emperor shall be born near Italy
> Who shall cost dear to the Empire.
> They shall remark on the company he keeps
> And he shall be thought of more as a butcher than a prince.[15]

And again:

> The thunderbolt shall strike his standard
> He shall die speaking proud words, great is the execution.
> The stone is in the tree, the proud nation yield,
> The monster purges his human frame by expiation.[16]

Hitler certainly saw to it that 'great was the execution', and he is certainly seen 'more as a butcher than a prince'. His political testament, written at the end of his life, is full of 'proud words' drenched in vitriol and hate. And, of course, the monster purged his human frame by suicide.

The final allusion to Hitler in Nostradamus, which is admittedly rather tenuous, is as follows:

> He shall have married a woman just before
> The divine wrath falleth on the great Prince.[17]

Hitler, it will be recalled, married Eva Braun not long before she joined him in death.

As can be seen from the account given in this chapter, the prophecies of Nostradamus are full of strange and thought-provoking references to the war. No wonder that both British and German propagandists seized upon them as powerful occult weapons. No wonder, moreover, that they resorted to forging Nostradamus prophecies when the genuine ones ran out! Of all the company of prophets and soothsayers, the figure of Nostradamus is by far the most remarkable.

14 Numbers and the Nazis

Numerology, the analysis of the meaning and application of numbers, particularly with regard to the way in which a person's destiny is bound up with his numbers, goes back to Pythagoras. Like other Greek philosophers of his day, he was concerned to find a principle of order within the universe. Pythagoras decided that the order is display was mathematical.

Numerologists are particularly concerned with the way in which an individual's birth and name-numbers vibrate together in a harmonious way. As one numerologist puts it, 'We live in a universe of vibrations and every person coming into the world has a vibration peculiar to the individual.' In the same way that colours are determined by different wavelengths of light, so many occultists in the nineteenth century believed in the idea of a vibrating universe. They claimed that everything vibrated at a given rate, and that the speed of vibration determined the nature of every individual entity. Occult forces were thus explained as being subtle rates of vibration. By analogy, they argued that the universe was a kind of giant harp. If we plucked its strings, every one of them would vibrate at its own note. The 'harp' has nine basic rates of vibration and that is why the numbers one to nine are so deeply significant. A person's name is what contains their true essence, but their date of birth is the moment at which the rate of vibration of the universe is inalienably fastened upon him and locked into his destiny.[1]

Pythagoras also discovered that the musical intervals known in his time – fourth, fifth and octave – could all be expressed as ratios between the numbers one to four. From this, Pythagoras concluded, like the numerologists after him, that the principle of

131

order within the universe was mathematical. This idea of his has come down to us as 'the music of the spheres'. Now the theory that everything in the universe is connected together in a single overall pattern is one of the most fundamental assumptions of magic.

For numerologists, the name of a person contains their fundamental essence. By converting names into numbers, we can discover the secrets of a person's inner nature and can determine whether or not their vibration is in harmony with the universe.[2] There are two basic ways of converting names into numbers. In the first system, each letter is written down in alphabetical order over a grid of numbers from 1 to 9. A–I are 1–9, J–R 1–9 again, and S–Z 1–8. In this system, the letters of the name Adolf Hitler add up to two.

The number two is traditionally a feminine number, 'twos' are regarded as having gentle natures, and capable of giving and receiving love. Other characteristics they are supposed to have are patience, quietness, a love of harmony and peace, and great powers of tact and mediation. They do not make good leaders and are almost always found to be excellent administrators. Persuasion rather than force is their method. They tend to be shy and weak-willed, although there is another side to them which can lead them to dark deeds of cruelty and mendacity. It is difficult, except in the second half of the last sentence, to recognize Hitler in this portrait at all. In general, though, I have always found this system to be deficient, and its older rival always strikes me as far more accurate.

The second system of numerology is Hebrew. It is far older, much more reliable, and can also be assimilated through what is known as '*notarikon*' and '*gematria*' with the even older occult learning of the Kabbalah. For these and many other reasons, it is vastly preferable to the system described above. In this method, a grid of only eight numbers is used. As the great clairvoyant, palmist and numerologist Cheiro said, the Hebrews did not use nine because, 'The ancient masters of occultism knew that in the Highest Sphere the number 9 represents the 9-lettered name of God.'[3]

The numbers on the Hebrew grid are arranged as follows:

1	2	3	4	5	6	7	8
A	B	C	D	E	U	O	F
I	K	G	M	H	V	Z	P
Q	R	L	T	N	W		
J		S			X		
Y							

As can be seen from the above grid,[4] in the Hebrew system of numerology the name Adolf Hitler adds up to seven,[5] not two as in the Western system. Seven, of course, is a 'sacred' number in most cultures throughout the world. It is the number of the saint, the philosopher, the occultist, the magician and the mystic. 'Sevens' are loners; they tend to keep themselves apart from the struggles of the world and meditate. They have no sense of humour and can be priggish. Money holds no interest for them and nor are they much bothered about physical comfort. On the whole, 'sevens' are clever, even brilliant, but they have another side to them which can irritate many people. As well as tending to be mysterious, imaginative, fey and dreamy, they can also be so bad at explaining themselves that they become incomprehensible, and are often deeply unhappy. 'Sevens' resent being questioned or disputed with and can become too easily depressed and discouraged. Pride and sarcasm are other weaknesses to which they are prone.

Even in this analysis there are certain traits which simply do not seem to fit with Hitler's character. However, on a closer examination the picture is not so clear-cut. For example, it may be difficult to imagine Hitler as being shy and retiring; and yet he was. Hitler on a public platform was a man transformed; but alone with a few people, he could be embarrassingly shy. Ebertin picked this up in his horoscope too, which is a further confirmation.

Although Hitler was anything but a saint, he could, when he began his magical studies, have chosen to use his gifts for good or evil. It was his own decision to follow the forces of darkness. The number seven does not direct destiny in itself; it only reveals the possibilities that lie within an individual. Hitler was not compelled to serve evil ends: he did so willingly.

Hitler was certainly a prig and a loner. Nor did money or comfort particularly interest him. And, indeed, the rest of the numerological analysis seems to fit Hitler very well indeed. And there is yet more to come. Not only was Hitler's name-number a seven, but he became the seventh member of the German Workers Party. As Cheiro, the greatest modern numerologist, says, in words that may be relevant here,

> Number 7 people have very peculiar ideas about religion. They dislike to follow the beaten track; they create a religion of their own, but one which appeals to the imagination and is based on the mysterious. These people usually have remarkable dreams and a great leaning to occultism; they have the gift of intuition, clairvoyance, and a peculiar magnetism of their own that has great influence over others.[6]

This seems to be a perfect description of Hitler.

Once you have determined your name-number, you must do all you can to make it vibrate harmoniously with everything else. Not only must you, if necessary, change your name to bring it into harmony with your birth-number; you must even do things on certain days which are more numerologically favourable than others. You must even be prepared to live elsewhere if the place you live is not in harmonious vibration with your own number.

The German navy took numerology extremely seriously, as they did any and every occult hypothesis that came their way. Some admirals actually spent days agonizing over the most conducive moment to launch destroyers and submarines, according to the principles of numerology.[7]

Curiously enough, Hitler was born on 20 April 1889. In Cheiro's interpretation of the Hebrew system – a version which he refers to as the Chaldaean system of numerology – only the 20th is regarded as the significant part of the birth number.[8] This being so, and adding up to two, which vibrates harmoniously to seven, it is not surprising, in numerological terms, that Hitler enjoyed early success. But both two and seven are ruled by the notoriously unstable moon – an interesting sidelight on Hitler's strong support for Hoerbiger's theory, perhaps. However, if we take the alternative system, and add up all the numbers in Hitler's birth-number, we arrive at the number five – which is also the number of *Der Führer*, Hitler's title. Five means a number of things to numerologists. In the first place, it is the number of sexuality and sensual enjoyment. 'Fives' are nervous, impatient, clever and restless. They are fascinated by the strange and the unusual. Travel and anything different attract them. More than any other number, they are prepared to take outrageous risks. They can be arrogant, sarcastic, adventurous and charismatic. They are rarely considerate or self-disciplined, and their sex urge can often manifest itself in perverse forms. Once again, this seems a strikingly true account of Hitler and his career.[9]

As we have already mentioned, one of the leading applications of numerology was in the field of the Kabbalah. Kabbalistic scholars believed that by the system of *gematria* they could discover both the character and destiny of any individual.

During the time of the Nazi rule, Kabbalists were eagerly searching the numbers for evidence of the future destiny of the world. Some Christians of a Kabbalistic bent discovered that the name Hitler could be made to fit the Number of the Beast in Revelation: 666.

Understandably, the Jewish Kabbalists were particularly concerned about Nazi activities. Using a method of *gematria* known as '*temurah*', which involves the use of anagrams and substitutions, they set their minds to work. The German army had just conquered Greece, and there was a large Jewish community in Syria which naturally feared the possibility of a German invasion. Since the Allies were still on the defensive at the time, the Jews turned to the Kabbalah for help. Spending the night in prayer and meditation, next morning the Kabbalists appeared to the anxious crowd with a message of hope. Having used the principles of *temurah*, they had managed to transpose the letters of the word 'Syria' into the word 'Russia'. At the time German–Soviet relations were perfectly calm; there was no hint of any prospect of tension between them, much less war. Yet, shortly after the Kabbalists had performed their magical ritual with the numbers, Hitler attacked Russia. 'And it came about just as they had provoked it by their magical art.'[10]

The plain facts, then, are as follows. In the first place, using the Hebrew system of numerology, we get a very plausible account of Hitler's character. Secondly, the Nazis, and in particular the German navy, were as obsessed with numerology as they were with all other forms of occultism. Finally, the Jewish Kabbalists may have decisively altered the outcome of the war by their use of *temurah*.

15 A Clash of Symbols

The swastika, both a token of good luck and an emblem of the sun, is one of the oldest human symbols. Another name for it is the 'fylfot'. It had always been used in the right-hand form, though occasionally the left-handed swastika was found, normally accompanying the workings of black magicians. Only in Tibet was it used in the left-hand form almost without exception. And, as we have seen, the connection between Tibet and the Nazis was very deep and devious indeed.

Another body of people who had extensive dealings with Tibet, and even believed that their own spirit masters came from there, was the Theosophical Society, whose founder, the bizarre Madame Blavatsky, we have encountered before. Like the Nazis, she was profoundly anti-Semitic and chose, for her own personal symbol, the left-hand or reverse swastika. Perhaps it is also significant that the title Blavatsky chose for the society's magazine was *Lucifer*.[1]

The Theosophical Society was extremely popular in Germany, and many of its members were keen Nazis. In the very same year that it was founded, the notorious racist and black magician Guido von List (again, previously mentioned) celebrated the summer solstice by a Satanic ritual which culminated in the burial of eight wine bottles in the pattern of a swastika.[2]

Since von List was one of the founding fathers of German nationalism in its occult-political form, he became a big influence on men who shared his views. Through his use of the swastika as a symbol of Aryan German occultism, it had spread widely into the circles of *völkisch* occultists. They disseminated its use into the German youth movements, and through them, it spread into the *Freikorps*, who adopted it as their symbol and even composed songs in its honour. One of these songs even celebrate the left-hand swastika.

Early in 1920 the German Workers Party was dissolved and reconstituted as the Nazi Party. Hitler decided that his new party needed an emblem and a flag to be its symbol. From all over Germany, occult-minded Nazis were busy working out designs for the party's symbol.

It was Hitler's association with the Thule Group which led to the choice of the reversed swastika as the Nazi Party emblem. The motif which Hitler eventually accepted was drawn up by a dentist called Dr Friedrich Krohn. Hardly surprisingly, he was a member of a secret occult order which ultimately derived from Lanz's Order of New Templars. Krohn came up with a white disk on a red background, in the centre of which was the swastika.

Krohn argued that the red stood for the party's new social order, white for its nationalism, and the swastika itself for the victory of Aryan man. As Krohn originally drew it, the swastika was facing the direction of the sun, the way by which it attracts good fortune and the powers of light. Hitler accepted the dentist's design but insisted on one small but vitally important change. Instead of the sunwise direction, Hitler instructed that the swastika should be reversed.

The swastika was itself a symbol derived originally from the East. Von List had already familiarized right-wing occultists with its normal pattern and the motif had become associated with Aryan and other occult-racist groupings. It was adopted by the Wandervogel and similar youth movements, and from them its use had filtered down into the *Freikorps*. But in the form which the Nazis adopted – the reversed swastika – it invokes not good fortune but the deliberate service of evil and black magic. This form of the swastika originated in Tibet, among the black orders of the Agarthi and Shamballah monks.

As has been said before in this book, magic in itself is morally neutral. It can be used for selfish or unselfish ends, in the service of kindness or the deliberate dedication of the magician to the service of evil. Hitler's act was a blatant advertisement to the world that the Nazi movement was a conscious turning-away

from the light, a deliberate worshipping – it is not too strong a
word – of the powers of darkness and evil.[3]

We have briefly touched upon Kabbalistic magic. In the
Kabbalah, there is a structure called the Tree of Life. This also
has an inverse side which is said by Kabbalists to be associated
with the Qlipoth, the Lords of Chaos. In magical theory, even
the powers of good can be perverted to the service of the
Qlipoth simply by reversing the symbols.[4]

Probably the most widely known example of this reversal of
symbols is the black mass. This relies on the belief that a normal
mass contains tremendous powers which can be turned to evil
purposes by reversing the symbols.[5]

Hitler was born and brought up into an orthodox Catholic
family. As we have already seen, when young he had been a
devout follower of his faith. Then he turned against it – not
towards atheism, but rather to an occult and magical complex of
ideas. He must, however, have been struck by the psychological
power of the mass, and it is significant that the ceremonies of the
Hitler Youth were too similar to the Catholic service for there to
be any question of coincidence.

There is also no doubt that under the influence of the sinister
figures of Eckart and Haushofer, Hitler took part in Satanic
ceremonies, and there are certainly significant hints to that
effect in the writings of Hitler and Rosenberg, both of whom
hated and despised Christianity. Even such a rationalist (relative
to Nazi standards!) as Martin Bormann said in 1941, 'National
Socialism and Christianity are irreconcilable.'[6] And Rosenberg
was even more scathing, in his series of published articles calling
for a National Reich Church. In these articles, Rosenberg spoke
of his determination to 'exterminate irrevocably' the 'strange
and foreign' faith of Christianity. Rosenberg demanded that the
Bible be suppressed in Germany. In its place, in the position of
honour on the altar of the new Reich Church, would be a new
'holy book' – *Mein Kampf*, of course. The National Reich
Church even had a series of articles, rather like the thirty-nine
articles of the Church of England. In the final one, Rosenberg
wrote, 'On the day of its foundation, the Christian cross must be
removed from all churches, cathedrals and chapels and it must
be superseded by the only unconquerable symbol, the swastika.'
And, of course, the swastika that Rosenberg wanted placed in

the churches was the left-hand swastika, the reversed symbol, the emblem of the powers of darkness.[7]

From the moment he achieved power in Germany, Hitler began a campaign of persecution against the Christian churches. His first anti-Christian action was, in 1933, to dissolve the Catholic Youth League. Only the Hitler Youth was permitted. All Catholic publications were soon being suppressed with an ardent zeal, and the following year the Nazis actually murdered the German chief of Catholic Action. In the years of Nazi rule, thousands of priests, monks, nuns and Catholic laymen were imprisoned and even murdered. Pope Pius XI spoke, with considerable alarm, about 'secret and open fundamental hostility to Christ and his Church'. The same treatment was also meted out to Protestants.[8] Indeed, there was such a strong conflict between the churches and the Party that it came to be a veritable clash of symbols: the cross, symbol of self-sacrifice, warred on the spiritual level with the left-hand swastika, symbol of the slavery to evil.

The swastika, among its other associations, represents the supreme deity – and by deliberately reversing the direction of its movement, the Nazis were openly honouring Satan. It is also the sign of the pole, and thus became linked by them with the myth of Thule, the origin of the dark initiates. It signifies the action of the originator of life upon the universe; and again, the Nazis' deliberate choice of the inverted swastika signified the action of Satan upon the world.[9]

The other sacred symbol that Rosenberg wanted to be placed in his National Reich Church, to the left of the altar, was the sword. This too has many meanings and associations, but one of its most obvious significations is of wounding and the power to wound. The sword is also the symbol of death, as the distaff is of life, and represents the spirit, death, psychic powers and destruction. It is not surprising, therefore, that the Nazis were drawn to its use as a powerful symbol of evil. It also conjures up visions of all-conquering heroes who serve the spirit, using the sword's powers to exterminate lesser beings – in fact, it has strong associations with rank, dignity and leadership. The symbolism of the sword is also linked to the ideas of the coldness of the metal and the heat of purifying fire. It represents the weapon which cuts off the realm of fire and the source of love from earth and the material world.[10]

The word 'sword', of course, is also linked with the word 'word', which, in turn, reminds us of Hitler's obsession with *Parsifal*. For in that book, von Eschenbach speaks of the word as a sword which comes out of the mouth of man. He speaks of a 'word-sword' which is rusty, broken and has lost its power. The word-sword can only be renewed and restored to its full and original state of power by discovering its source. 'If your mouth did learn the words,' von Eschenbach says, 'the power of fortune will sprout and grow forever.' Hitler had obviously studied *Parsifal* deeply, and this reference to the powers of the word must have influenced his decision to make the fullest use of all his own powers of oratory. But, where von Eschenbach speaks of the need for humility and compassion, Hitler chose instead to elevate the dark side of the sword and the word, preferring mastery over men to self-discipline and the betterment of humanity.[11]

In 1908 von List formed a secret society of initiates to study the runes, an early European form of the modern Roman alphabet. Von List claimed that the runes were derived directly from an arcane group of German magicians who dated back as far as Arminius, the German chieftain who had beaten the Roman army in the time of Augustus. He argued that this occult order had left clues to its existence in place-names, among German mystical and occult writings and in the stained-glass windows of Gothic churches. He subscribed to the ideas of the mysterious Fulcanelli, who claimed that the Gothic churches conveyed, through a hidden code, the secrets of alchemy. Von List claimed that these could be decoded and would open the way to the transmutation of base metals into gold, the nostrum which would heal all ills, and the elixir of life. Such men as Paracelsus, Boehme and the German mystic Meister Eckhart – not to be confused with Dietrich Eckart – knew the secret, and their writings could be decoded by fellow initiates, using the methods of the runes.[12] Members of von List's secret society later infiltrated the Nazis; and, curiously enough, the runes became one of the SS's chief preoccupations.

Mention of the powers of an ancient alphabet leads us back to the word-sword. Words were seen by the Nazi initiates as being the primary link between matter and thought. Through the utterance of certain words of power, changes could be brought about on the material plane. They also believed that the alphabet could be derived from the study of the stars, in that particular letters were related to particular heavenly bodies. There was great emphasis on the sun and moon, which were felt to have a profound effect upon human destiny and especially upon the evolution of language and the alphabet.[13]

Runes, the alphabet, Fulcanelli and alchemy were all related together to the sword and the swastika. Hardly an occult theory escaped the attention of the Nazis, especially in Himmler's Occult Bureau and the German navy. It cannot be stressed too often that the world as perceived by the Nazis was a magical cosmos. As such, anything which could assist them in their aims of world domination through magical means was eagerly grasped. And in every case, where the choice existed between a positive and negative symbol, the Nazis opted for the negative, evil version. In this respect they demonstrated their consistent adherence to a conscious and deliberate Satanism, an attempt to establish a religion of blood and destruction. Only because other, positive and beneficial occult influences fought against them was it possible to overcome them. Probably at no time in recent history has the world come closer to falling under the domination of a group of initiates serving consciously Satanic ends.[14]

If we cast our minds back to the scene in the Habsburg Treasure House, with both Stein and Hitler standing before the Spear of Destiny, we can perhaps understand how strange powers can intervene from time to time in human affairs. One has only to contrast the humility and love which Stein felt in the presence of the Spear with the arrogance, hatred and lust for power which it evoked in Hitler, to realize at once that there is a profound difference between a black magician and a white one. Stein worked for the power of good, serving the light; while Hitler attempted to plunge the world into a state of total and permanent darkness. As with the word-sword, so too the Spear has the power to heal or to slay. No clearer indication of Hitler's Satanism can be given than his determination to use the very spear said to have pierced the side of Christ as the channel for a dark current, which came close to ending civilization on Earth. Between Stein's way of viewing the Spear and Hitler's there could, indeed, be no compromise. One either serves the light or the dark forces. Hitler consciously and deliberately sought to serve the powers of darkness and evil.[15]

16 Black Camelot

Of all the Nazi leaders, Himmler was probably the furthest removed from reality, in spite of severe competition. A man without feelings or imagination, he was utterly lacking in personality, and seemed totally unaware of the world around him. Essentially passive and negative by nature, he seemed to have no life of his own.

As Willi Frischauer put it in his biography of Himmler, 'Himmler has been compared with a length of wire whose electric current is supplied from outside – that current being Hitler. He himself could not supply any current.'[1] General Guderian once described him as like a man from another planet, while another acquaintance remarked that he had 'a touch of the robot' about him. Even Rosenberg, the Nazi Party ideologist, could never look him in the eye. There was, in fact, something altogether inhuman and chilling about Himmler that surpassed the worst monsters in the Party – even Hitler. For the latter chose to offer his soul in the service of evil; but Himmler had no soul to call his own.

From boyhood Himmler had been brought up on German mythology and the great heroes of German history. This weedy specimen of a man, who was rejected by the German navy during World War I for being physically and mentally unfit for service, was incapable of love or any other normal human feeling. His schoolmates looked upon him as an utter nobody, though they also despised him for being a notorious sneak.

When the First World War was over, Himmler went to Munich Technical College to study agriculture, and then became a representative for a firm which manufactured fertilizer. This turn of events deeply depressed him, for he had grandiose hopes and dreams for a glowing future.

During his student days Himmler discovered the infant Nazi Party. With typical *naïveté* he tried to join the SA, but the battle-hardened Storm-Troopers had no use for a dreamy, weedy-looking man with glasses and a girlish voice. Contemptuously, they rejected him. But Himmler did not give up his determination to be accepted by one of the various *Freikorps* groups. At last, his persistence paid off: one of the smallest and least significant of the patriotic militias allowed him to join them.

Standing in uniform with his fellow militiamen, Himmler felt a sense of pride in himself at last. But destiny was to hold far higher things for him than this. The first step on his ladder to success was the Munich *putsch*, during which his unit came out in support of Hitler, and Himmler himself stayed as part of a picket outside the War Ministry. When the police came at last, they broke up the picket and arrested its members, with one exception. Nobody thought the insignificant Himmler was worth arresting. They did not even bother to confiscate his pistol. Even with a loaded gun, Himmler was totally unable to attract attention. Eventually, he caught a train back home and retreated into anonymity once more. But the aftermath of the *putsch* was to give Himmler his first opportunity. The SA was banned by the authorities and when Hitler was released from prison he raised a new force to replace it, the SS.[2]

By this time Himmler had been sacked from his job, and started looking for a post more in line with his ambitions. He applied for the position of secretary to Gregor Strasser, at that time the head of the Nazi Party in Landshut. Strasser offered Himmler the job, in spite of his stammer, his general puniness and lack of personality – largely because the latter had graduated in chemistry and Strasser had been a chemist before he became a full-time politician. From now on Himmler's star began to rise, as Strasser too rose in the party hierarchy. As Strasser became propaganda chief of the Nazis, so Himmler too began to move, almost unnoticed, nearer to the levers of power.[3]

Meanwhile the SS had comparatively little to do at that moment. They supplemented their activities as Hitler's personal bodyguard by selling advertising space in the Party newspaper.

They also gathered information about the activities of opponents of the Party, and Himmler, as secretary to Strasser, had the job of filing and co-ordinating the information received. So efficiently did Himmler perform these duties that he was soon elevated to the post of assistant chief of propaganda. In spite of this promotion, Hitler then regarded Himmler with total contempt. He would not even talk to him, though in his office Himmler kept a portrait of Hitler with which he held repeated conversations. It was perhaps Hitler's warped sense of humour, then, that led him in 1925, after the ban on the SA had been lifted, and the need for the SS seemed to have disappeared altogether, to appoint the glorified filing clerk to the post of deputy leader of the SS.[4]

At the time this was seen by every Nazi leader as a hilarious practical joke by Hitler. But Himmler did not see it that way at all. In addition to his grand but meaningless title, Himmler also received the 'blood-flag', the Nazi flag brandished during the failed Munich *putsch*. To Hitler, it was a practical joke; but not to Himmler. Hitler had no idea that he would have to break the power of the SA and murder its leadership soon after taking power. But he was soon to have cause to change his mind about Himmler.[5]

Within a short time, Himmler turned the SS into an elite corps, smartly turned-out, well drilled, with membership being restricted to those who exemplified 'Aryan ideals'. Hitler had no higher opinion of Himmler's character than before; but he did have cause to reassess his abilities. Before long Himmler had been allowed to increase the strength of the SS from what had been a small bodyguard for the Führer to a force of 30,000 armed and trained men. And so, largely as the result of a frivolous prank by Hitler, Himmler became the organizer of one of the most hideous reigns of terror in human history.

When Hitler took power in 1933, and found to his cost that he had to deal with the SA, it was to Himmler and his SS troops that he turned. In late 1933 Himmler assumed responsibility for the political police – the Gestapo – in every German province except Prussia. With the SS and the Gestapo both under his control, Himmler was now one of the most powerful men in Germany, and soon to become one of the most feared. During the massacre of the SA, the event which became popularly known as 'the Night of the Long Knives', Himmler personally supervised the firing squads. One of the men shot in cold blood on his orders was his own former boss Gregor Strasser, the man without whom he would never have been a force in German politics. Himmler even noted down the names of any SS men who were unwise enough to feel remorse at this orgy of unbridled killing.[6]

In addition to cold-blooded murder of former colleagues, Himmler was also responsible for the introduction into Germany of concentration camps. Under an order euphemistically dubbed 'protective custody', hundreds of people were arrested without trial and sent to concentration camps. In a nauseating example of the hypocrisy which he added to his lack of common humanity, Himmler, in the same year he had personally founded Dachau camp, made a public speech in which he said, 'Protective custody is an act of care. You must understand there was hostility against those who opposed us. Only by taking them under protective custody was I able to save these personalities who have caused this annoyance. Only in this way was I able to guarantee their security of health and life.'[7]

Nor did Himmler stop at the murder, torture and enslavement of millions of men, women and children. He even got manufacturers to come up with such loathsome devices as radium-ray machines to sterilize the unsuspecting workers in the camps as they filled in forms at counters. The brain of this man was so twisted that he did not even take pleasure in such acts, as a sadist might have done. If Himmler had been asked to save 6 million Jews he would probably have done it in exactly the same spirit of robotic obedience.

Like Hitler, Himmler was obsessed with the Spear of Destiny legends[8] – so obsessed, in fact, that in 1935 he had a replica of the Spear made for himself, in an attempt to realize an old German prophecy which warned of 'a gigantic storm which would appear out of the East to overwhelm the German peoples if it was not confronted and turned back in the region of the Birkenwald in Westphalia'.[9] Himmler interpreted this to mean that the Russians would invade and conquer Germany unless they were met by a dedicated order along the lines of the old Teutonic Knights. These knights had been on crusades and adhered to the highest ideals of noble chivalry. But chivalry was not in the nature of the order of dark initiates which Himmler had in mind.[10]

Himmler conceived the idea of the SS becoming an inner elite of men serving the blood, who should be able to prove pure Aryan descent for at least five generations. For their headquarters, he wanted to build a castle in Westphalia, staffed by this same inner sanctum. Out of this castle would step forth the new Teutonic Knights, but this time men whose ideals were not the chivalrous ones of service and courtesy, but those which glorified strength and the Aryan blood.[11]

On the ruins of an ancient medieval fort, Himmler laid the foundation stone of what was to become known as the Wewelsburg. Its less flattering nickname among SS members was Black Camelot. This castle was built by hundreds of slave workers from a concentration camp, who worked on starvation rations and cowered under the whips of the SS guards. They built a palace for Himmler's dark initiates.

> Every room [Frischauer tells us], was furnished in a different style – not even a single desk was duplicated. Only leading craftsmen of every branch had been employed to produce fine tapestries, solid oak furniture, wrought-iron door handles, candlesticks. Priceless carpets were acquired, curtains of heavy brocade flanked the high windows. Doors were carved and embellished with precious metals and stones. Built in the old Germanic style on a triangular foundation, the burg's towers rose high over the surrounding forest.[12]

In addition to the sheer splendour of the Wewelsburg, Himmler ordered that each room be designed to exemplify the life and work of all the individuals who had been associated with the Spear of Destiny throughout its long history. One room, the Frederick Barbarossa room, was always locked, reserved for the use of Hitler himself. Himmler himself had the exclusive use of the Henry the Fowler room, the man of whom he believed himself to be the physical reincarnation. In this room, where Himmler slept when he was staying at the Wewelsburg, he kept the replica of the Spear of Destiny.[13]

In this Black Camelot, a Satanic coven of thirteen dark initiates, presided over by Himmler himself, were mocked the chivalrous ideals of the Teutonic Knights in their own obscenely perverted parody of knighthood. The order's initiation was known as 'the ceremony of the stifling air', from the psychic atmosphere in which it took place. At the height of the ritual, a black mass was performed in accordance with the traditions of Satanism.[14] All thirteen dressed in black, carried daggers and wore signet rings of solid silver, inscribed with intricate magical sigils. Each man had a coat-of-arms and a seat allotted to him at a round table, a grim echo of the Arthurian legend. There, they waited for their Grand Master, Himmler, to begin his ministrations. Sometimes they would sit and meditate, but more often, under the personal direction of Himmler, they would engage in magical rituals and spells, and try to contact the 'Racial Soul'. On occasions of special solemnity they would sit at the round table and evoke the help of Satanic entities in their deadly work of black magic.[15]

Beneath the castle lay the SS crypt, known as the 'realm of the dead'. Here, twelve pedestals were set round a stone hollow. If one of the inner circle of thirteen died, their coat-of-arms was to be burned and stored in an urn on top of one of the pedestals for the edification of their successors.

Out of what had once been simply Hitler's personal bodyguard, Himmler set out to create a magical order of dedicated men, serving the ends of National Socialism.

Karl Ernst, who at one time headed the rival SA organization, once referred contemptuously to Himmler as a 'black Jesuit'. Nor was this mere irony, for Himmler's order was modelled specifically on the Society of Jesus – the Jesuits – or a sinister version thereof.[16] As the Jesuits owed allegiance only to the Pope, so the SS was answerable only to Hitler. As the Jesuits for a time actually enjoyed their own state in Paraguay, so Himmler's plans for the SS after the expected German victory in the war included the resurrection of the ancient kingdom of Burgundy. Burgundy would have been an independent model SS state, with its own army, police force, government and embassy in Berlin.[17] St Ignatius Loyola, founder of the Jesuits, ran his order with a general in charge, assisted by four administrators; Himmler had himself – the *Reichsführer* – and four heads of department to assist him. Even Hitler called Himmler 'my Loyola'. And, like the Jesuits, the SS made extensive use of a key magical technique known as visualization.

In spite of the differences in what was prayed for, the actual techniques used by the Jesuits were more or less the same as those adopted by Himmler and the SS.

Bearing all this in mind, Himmler's frequent conversations with Hitler's portrait start to look less ridiculous and rather more sinister. Was Himmler, we wonder, using the portrait to create magical visualizations in order to influence Hitler? Himmler may have been using the picture to reach out and make magical contact with the mind of Hitler. We know that Hitler himself made extensive use of visualization to assist him in controlling people and situations. Even during the war he spent hours trying to create phantom armies to fight the Allies. Is it likely that '*der treue Heinrich*', with his own extensive occult preoccupations and his loyalty to Hitler, would not also be familiar with and use extensively one of the most fundamental and basic magical techniques?[18]

Himmler always claimed that the SS was an elite within the Nazi Party. As early as the 1920s he made a speech in which he remarked, 'The SA is the infantry of the line, the SS is the guard. There has always been a guard. The SS will become the imperial guard of the new Germany.' By 1933, however, with power at last at his disposal, Himmler's ideas about the SS became even more elitist. From an imperial guard he set out to transform it into an order of knighthood.[19]

As a first step in this process all SS members had to produce a family tree free of Jewish ancestors back to 1900, and the officers had to provide one as far back as 1750. At times, in the case of important officers, this rule was relaxed. The most famous example was Himmler's deputy, Heydrich, who until his eventual assassination was the second most powerful man in the SS, in spite of his Jewish blood. Himmler himself had Jewish relatives by marriage and until the last stages of the Final Solution managed to keep them free from persecution.

It took three years to be accepted as a full member of the SS, before which a sort of probationary period had to be served by the recruit. At the end of the three-year 'novitiate' the recruit had to undergo a catechism of political and religious questioning. At the end of this he would be sent to serve, first in the Labour Corps and later in the army. Only then was he granted full membership of the SS and permitted to wear the ceremonial dagger. All SS members had to participate regularly in the various magical ceremonies, based on old Teutonic worship of Woden, which Himmler himself had devised.[20]

Himmler's belief that he was the reincarnation of the Saxon king Henry the Fowler led him to hold long conversations with the king's spirit. How Himmler could commune with his own previous incarnation is a moot point; but logic and consistency were never his strong points. The form of reincarnation in which Himmler believed was derived from Karl Eckhart, who taught that we are reborn in the bodies of our own descendants, so that we will all become our own ancestors. I have not come across this form of reincarnation anywhere else, but it seems to have impressed Himmler sufficiently for him to order 20,000 copies of Eckhart's book on the subject for the use of the SS.[21] About this time Himmler began to be referred to – behind his back, naturally – as 'the Grand Master of German occultism'.

Himmler required members of the SS to attend ceremonies in worship of the Hammer of Thor, among other things. He also substituted the summer solstice for Christmas as the chief 'holy day' – if one dares to use such a phrase – and presented his members with midsummer presents. All services of marriage, baptism and burial were, in the case of SS members, performed, not by a priest or vicar, but by the local SS commander. Himmler also believed strongly in polygamy, and intended to introduce it if the Germans won the war. 'Marriage as it is today,' he declared, 'is the Satanic work of the Roman Catholic Church. Our present marriage laws are absolutely immoral. After the war monogamy will cease to be enforced upon promiscuous mankind. The racially pure blood of German heroes will be transmitted to as many offspring as possible.[22]

There were, of course, many other involvements by Himmler in occult activities throughout his career. Those that we have not chronicled already will be dealt with briefly in some of the remaining chapters.

17 Bumps on the Head

Phrenology, the practice of interpreting a person's character and abilities by studying the shape of his or her head and particularly the bumps upon it, was a subject of particular interest to Himmler and the SS occultists in the Nazi Occult Bureau. It began as a development of physiognomy, the determination of character by the study of the face. Unlike physiognomy, however, phrenology was bound up in the complex of discredited ideas known as faculty psychology, which put forward the thesis that every human capacity could be assigned a specific location within the brain.

Phrenology was founded by an Austrian anatomist, Franz Gall, in the late 1700s. Gall specialized in neurology and decided that the activities of the mind were 'epiphenomena', or by-products, of the brain. Such a materialist account of thought was unacceptable in Catholic Austria, and Gall was soon expelled from the country.[1]

Before long Gall had developed his basic idea into a whole system: phrenology. Gall believed that if an ability was well developed in a person, the part of the brain to which it was referred must also be well developed. The other component of his system was the idea that bumps and dents upon the head corresponded with similar bulges in the brain. Gall asserted that there were exactly thirty-three of these organs, corresponding to the appropriate mental faculties.[2] Thus, for instance, he claimed that the faculty of memory was located just behind the eyes.

In his own time, Gall's work was treated as an amusing parlour game; but the efforts of his disciple Spurzheim in the early 1800s made phrenology seem more plausible. Spurzheim added another four organs to Gall's, making thirty-seven in all. He argued that phrenology could be used to detect crime and to prevent corrupt politicians from taking office by taking readings from their heads. His efforts came so close to making the subject respectably scientific that phrenological societies sprung up all over Britain and the United States. Spurzheim's successor George Coombe managed to persuade Queen Victoria to allow him to examine the heads of her children. Even the hard-headed Wallace, co-discoverer of evolution with Darwin, decided that phrenology was true.[3]

However, its days were numbered. As its opponents began empirical testing, they discovered people whose character was exactly opposite to what the phrenologists said it should be. Anatomists were also able to establish that the bumps upon a person's head were nothing to do with faculties, but simply indicated physical features upon the skull. As the scientific community rejected phrenology, so the occultists took it up.[4]

Wandering hypnotists took to adding phrenology to their performances; the results were, of course, no more than the result of suggestion. From this 'hypnophrenology' a branch of alternative medicine, known as phreno-magnetism, came into being. This involved hypnotizing the patient and then stroking the faculty believed to be affected with a magnet. Under the influence of the occultists who took it up, phrenology ceased to be the materialistic science which Gall and Spurzheim had considered it to be. Instead, phrenological divination became a matter of the psychic sensitivity of the individual operator. It was no longer a case of an exact correspondence of faculties, but of the ability of the person 'reading' the head to intuit the character of the sitter. As such, it became more an exercise in clairvoyance than a scientific discovery.[5]

Predictably, once phrenology had become an occult discipline instead of a scientific one, it attracted the attention of Himmler. Before long he was insisting that all members of the SS study and pay attention to phrenology, and it soon became one of the major occult preoccupations of the SS. Then the 'science' was entangled with the racial mythology of Nazism. Phrenological 'arguments' were produced to demonstrate such things as the natural superiority of Aryans to all other examples of humanity.

The occultist who seems to have been responsible for this

development of a racial phrenology was, not surprisingly, the Austrian von List. He saw phrenology as one more example of the hidden knowledge which bands of German initiates had preserved through the centuries. Von List's 'Armanen Order' studied phrenology with an Aryan slant. Before long they were finding in it exactly what they had wanted to find. Through von List, this phrenological racism passed via a splinter group called the Germanen Order into Himmler and the SS.[6]

All candidates for the Germanen Order had to have their heads measured to make sure that they fulfilled the criteria for being truly Aryan. A phrenological analysis of each member's character and 'racial soul' was then conducted.[7] This obsession with measuring skulls was also to become standard practice within the SS. Not only members, but also victims of its senseless brutality had to submit to the charade of skull measurement. Jews, Bolsheviks, Slavs and other 'racially inferior elements' were all subjected to this pointless and degrading pseudo-scientific hocus-pocus.[8]

Phrenology, according to the Nazis, enabled them to determine not only the relationship between particular faculties and physical indications upon a person's head, but also, by such things as the size and shape and weight of the skull to determine the relative 'brain-power' of both individuals and different racial groups. No one familiar with the Nazis' racial mythology will be in the least bit surprised to hear that 'Nordic' skulls were always found superior to those of Jews, Slavs, Bolsheviks and everyone else.

According to phrenologists, the brain is divided into five zones. These are further divided into 33 organs (according to Gall), 37 (Spurzheim's estimate) or 40 (Coombe). The back of the head – interestingly linked with the Qoph, a Kabbalistic path of somewhat dubious nature – governs such things as sex drive, fertility and friendship. On either side of the head the animal zones are found. These govern such things as greed, anger, self-indulgence and destructiveness. The zone of prudence is formed by a band from ear to ear over the crown of the head, which contains the organs of secrecy, pride, conscientiousness, self-esteem and desire for the approval of others. The moral zone is situated at the top of the head, and stretches forward from the crown to the hair-line. It rules such things as kindness, spirituality, hope, reverence and idealism. The front of the head, especially the temples, eyes and forehead, governs the intellectual zone.[9]

It is interesting to speculate on how well developed certain organs were among Nazi leaders. Hitler, for example, must have had overdeveloped animal zones. And his moral zone must have been virtually non-existent. Either the Nazis did not interpret the data in this manner or the results they obtained by phrenology bore no relation to the real world. In either event, they failed to demonstrate that phrenology, as a guide to abilities and actions, was a system worth following. Spurzheim, who had advocated cranial measurement as a means of avoiding corruption in public office, would have been horrified to see the use to which Himmler and the SS put his supposedly rational and humane system of character analysis.

Under the Nazis virtually any and every item of rejected 'knowledge' was absorbed into the Occult Bureau and at least examined with a view to its possible truth and usefulness. Phrenology, which had begun life as a totally materialistic attempt to explain mental faculties in terms of brain functions and their location in specific areas of the skull, became in the hands of the SS a lunatic occult-racial project dedicated to the demonstration of the innate superiority of Aryan man to other representatives of the human race.[10]

Although phrenologists still survive to this day, they are among the rarest of occult practitioners.[11] And never since have they enjoyed the same 'scientific' standing that they enjoyed under the patronage of Himmler and his Satanic cohorts of SS men. Without phrenology, some of the more bizarre and disgusting Nazi experiments might never have been carried out. That is hardly the fault of the originators of phrenology; but it highlights one of the basic flaws in the system, its capacity to be interpreted in various ways by different practitioners. When linked with some of Himmler's other occult obsessions, phrenology somehow seems vaguely sinister in itself. Perhaps this is only to be expected. All forms of faculty psychology lend themselves exceptionally well to the service of totalitarianism; for all such states adopt an essentially reductionist approach to life. One is not a fully-rounded man or woman of potentially infinite complexity; one is a Jew or a Negro, a Bolshevik or a Capitalist. In such a mental atmosphere, the acceptance that a doctrine like phrenology obtained under the Nazis should perhaps not occasion us any real surprise.

18 Among Murderers and Madmen

From the very beginning of Nazi rule the anti-Semitic obsessions of their occult-racial schemes always threatened the possibility of the Final Solution. It is but a small step from measuring heads to demonstrate the inferiority of other races to doing so with the intention of murdering them – all for the sake of some perverted ideal of racial purity. At first, though, simple unsystematic massacre and brutality was the method. By 1941, however, more sinister counsels were at work.

In that year Professor August Hirt, head of the Anatomical Institute of Strasbourg University, wrote a letter of complaint to Himmler's office. Although the institute had a large collection of human skulls from most races, he explained, they were extremely short of representatives from the Jewish nation. Since the Germans were now engaged in a war against the Soviet Union, it would now be possible to remedy this defect. Large numbers of 'Jewish-Bolshevik commissars' should be captured alive. After measuring their heads, they should then be killed in ways that did not damage the skulls in any way. Their heads should then be severed from their bodies and sent off to the Strasbourg Institute in a hermetically sealed tin can.

Any normal person would have been disgusted at this appalling suggestion, but Himmler was enthusiastic about the idea. He saw to it that Hirt got the skulls he needed for his 'anthropological measurements'.[1]

It was not enough, Hirt added, simply to use the skulls of those 'Jewish Bolsheviks' who had died in battle: the victims' heads should be measured while they were still alive; only after should they be murdered in cold blood. Before long Hirt was

155

adding to his monstrous demands: not just skulls but whole skeletons were required, he decided. 'Jewish-Bolshevik' prisoners, numbering 109, were delivered to a concentration camp and subjected to the degrading farce of 'anthropological measurement'. Then they were stripped naked and gassed. The bodies were sent to Hirt, still warm. But the monstrous professor still had the audacity to complain that 'in view of the vast amount of scientific research still involved the task of reducing the corpses to skeletons has not yet been completed'.[2]

Again in 1941, more appalling experiments were begun as the result of the promptings of a quack doctor called Rascher, who had come to Himmler's attention as a result of his wife's astonishing fertility. Between the ages of forty-eight and fifty-two she had, so it appeared, given birth to three children. In reality, the children had been kidnapped from orphanages, but Rascher maintained the pretence.[3]

Rascher received a letter of congratulation from Himmler about his wife's fertility and responded by asking the SS leader for permission to use 'criminals' in medical 'research'. Rascher wanted to study the effect of high altitude upon fliers but had been unable to obtain volunteers because of the high probability of death occurring during the experiments. As with Hirt's 'anthropological measurements', so with Rascher's 'altitude testing' – Himmler was delighted to assist. He saw to it that Rascher received concentration camp inmates, who were promptly put into a decompression chamber in high-altitude simulation tests. No oxygen was supplied, and of course all the subjects died. The scientific value of the 'experiments' was nil and the needless suffering inflicted upon them was as pointless as it was unforgivable.[4] However, after a year of these insane and cruel experiments, Rascher moved on to another revolting programme.

In the earlier experiments he had killed his subjects in a decompression chamber and then frozen their bodies. Now he moved on to examine ways of reviving those who had come close to death by freezing. These 'freezing-experiments' involved naked prisoners being placed on a stretcher outside the barracks at evening. They were covered with a sheet, and every hour a bucket of cold water would be poured over them. Later Rascher decided that the sheet should be removed and the prisoner should simply lie on the stretcher naked, the cold water being poured over his naked body. The monstrous doctor even had the appalling effrontery to complain to Himmler about the difficulty of getting his victims sufficiently cold. He wrote to Himmler and said, 'Thank God we have had some really cold weather at Dachau.'[5] As the German philosopher Schopenhauer remarked in a different context in 1838, 'How is it possible to be so lacking in compassion?'

One eyewitness describes how two Russian officers were made to strip naked and get into a cold-water tank. Rascher refused repeated appeals from prisoners and even one or two guards to give them a lethal injection. 'After three hours one of the Russians said to his companion, "Comrade, ask the officer to shoot us." But he only replied that he did not expect any mercy from a Nazi. Then they shook hands with a "Farewell, Comrade" ' the eyewitness concluded. It took five hours before death mercifully intervened.[6]

The reason for these lunatic 'experiments' was to satisfy a theory of Himmler's concerning 'animal heat'. In deference to Himmler's wishes, Rascher investigated the superiority of 'animal heat' in reviving people over other methods. As a result, concentration camp inmates were first subjected to the atrocities described above and then laid upon a bed between two naked women transferred from brothel service. Himmler believed that the attraction between the sexes released a 'vital force' from the partners: 'animal heat'. Once the poor victims were revived they found themselves lying between two naked women and were instructed to have intercourse with them. About half of them actually managed to achieve this. Rascher reported that 'after coitus there ensued a very rapid rise in temperature'.[7]

Rascher had actually experienced pangs of conscience at the beginning of this hideous commission. But it was not due to the loathsome nature of what he had been asked to do, rather that one of the prostitutes supplied to him was 'Aryan'. Rascher declared indignantly, 'My racial conscience is outraged by the prospect of exposing to racially inferior concentration camp elements a girl who is outwardly pure Nordic. For this reason I decline to use this girl for my experimental purposes.' Sadly, a non-Aryan prostitute was found and the experiments upon the unfortunate prisoners recommenced.

As a supreme touch, Rascher discovered – after conducting goodness only knows how many of these horrific experiments – that hot-water baths were superior to animal heat as a means of reviving frozen people. Himmler refused to accept this and insisted upon more tests being carried out. Rascher at first simply refused, saying, 'It has been proven that quick heating has in each case been more efficacious than slow heating, since the body temperature still keeps on sinking after the body has been removed from the cold water. Heating by animal warmth – animals, or female bodies – would take too long.' But Himmler still refused to accept Rascher's conclusion. Rascher was instructed to continue with his experiments in animal warmth together with other methods. How many human beings were sacrificed to Himmler's insane belief in the superiority of naked female bodies as a reviving agent over normal methods we shall never know for certain. But even Rascher knew from an early stage that they were scientifically valueless. Yet – an order from Himmler could not be lightly disobeyed, so more and more people were made to suffer needlessly to prove the truth of the demonstrably false 'animal warmth' idea.[8]

We now turn to examine the ironic way in which Steiner, the Nazi's greatest occult opponent, was unintentionally instrumental in aspects of the Final Solution.

Count Hermann Keyserling, a German philosopher who owned estates in Silesia, was being troubled by rabbits. They had bred to such proportions that they were overrunning his farmlands and none of the conventional methods of control worked. In early 1924 he convened a conference on what would nowadays be called 'alternative' methods of dealing with vermin. He told the local peasants and small farmers that he would demonstrate a new form of pest control which would get rid of the rabbits within three days.[9]

The man who came to Keyserling's estates to perform the task was Steiner. His first act was to shoot a male rabbit and bring it into a laboratory. The spleen, genital organs and part of the skin were removed. These were then burned, and the ashes mixed with various homeopathic remedies. The result of this activity, Steiner claimed, would be that the rabbits would be alarmed into leaving their present habitat. Spread out into the wind, the rabbit ashes were dispersed all over the estate.[10]

Nothing happened for two whole days. But on the third day thousands of rabbits were sniffing excitedly at an old ash tree. Running up and down, they sniffed the air in obvious alarm. More and more rabbits came to join them at the ash tree, leaving their homes as if they had suddenly become a threat to their very existence. By nightfall the entire rabbit population had fled, in a state of nervous panic, in a north-eastern direction towards the distant wastelands. It was many years before a single rabbit set foot on the Keyserling estates.[11]

Unfortunately, Steiner's experiments were to be repeated years later with altogether more sinister intentions and results. The 'potentised' ashes of the spleen, testicles and parts of the skin of Jewish males were also burnt to ashes in an attempt to drive the last remaining Jews out of Germany for good. The order to perform this action came from Hitler, but its conception sprang from the warped brain of Himmler.[12]

From Hitler, Himmler had learned about homeopathic remedies. Before long he had discovered the accounts of Steiner's experiments and conceived a diabolically sinister plan in his own mind. If rabbits could be controlled in this way, Himmler reasoned, why should it not be possible to treat the Jews in the same way? A whole branch of the Nazi Occult Bureau was set up to investigate the possibilities.[13]

In 1943 Himmler ordered the first experiments to be carried out on human subjects. Before then, rats had been used. Jews at Buchenwald were injected with the potentised ashes of male Jews. These experiments went on until 1945. The SS, on Himmler's instructions, scattered Jewish ashes from the concentration camps across the entire land of Germany. Even with the Allied armies driving on deep into Germany itself, the SS was still carrying out these disgusting experiments.[14]

Another fringe medicine obsession of Himmler and indeed the Nazi occultists generally was what the Victorians called 'eugenics'. This aimed at the selective breeding of a superior race and the gradual elimination of inferior racial elements. An SS doctor wrote to Himmler in a fever of excitement. He had discovered a plant, he wrote, which induced irreversible sterility but without otherwise injuring the patient. This would enable the Reich to use the Bolsheviks and Jews as slave labour, but without any danger of their breeding. Himmler was as excited by the news as the quack doctor who had disgraced his calling by bringing its possibilities to his attention. At once he gave orders for its experimental use on 'Jewish-Bolshevik elements'. It seems that, no matter how barbarous the men in charge of the machinery of death and destruction were, their helpers were just as eager to assist them in their lunatic ends. In their own way, the concentration camp doctors were even more evil and depraved than the monsters they served.[15]

Within a year of this kind of mad systematic cruelty, Haushofer fell from favour as a result of his World Ice Theory Bureau's inaccurate weather forecasts for the Russian campaign. The new guru became the sinister Hielscher, who somehow managed to slip through the net at Nuremberg when other Nazis were put on trial for their crimes against humanity. Under Hielscher's malignant influence, Hitler pushed on to a new phase in his insanity – the Final Solution. Under this programme, the deliberate and systematic extermination of Jews for the 'crime' of being non-Aryan was put into operation. No one will ever know the exact numbers of people who suffered death at the hands of the absurd Nazi occult-racial theories, but the Poles – who were also deemed an inferior race – lost a quarter of their population; the Romanies, again seen as racially inferior, lost around a million people; and the Jews, of course, had six million of their people murdered. All in all, the numbers of victims sacrificed to the occult-racial Nazi mythology was around 10 to 12 million.[16]

But the extermination of races believed to be inferior, horrifying and disgusting as it is, has been well documented already. It is hard to dwell long in this miasmal swamp of men who seemed incapable of distinguishing between right and wrong, kindness and cruelty. Let us turn now from the murderers and study the madmen. Often, of course, they were one and the same.

Another obsessive preoccupation of Himmler was the Lebensborn, the SS maternity organization. Like much else in Nazi doctrine, this was also anticipated by the monstrous Lanz. Lanz urged the necessity of setting up human-breeding farms so that Aryans – particularly Germans – could mate with other Aryans and thus 'eradicate Slavic and Alpine elements from Germanic heredity'. Lanz's idea was enthusiastically taken up by Himmler and put under the direction of the SS. The Lebensborn became a human stud-farm at which unfortunate German and Nordic girls were compelled to satisfy as many men of Aryan extraction as wished to avail themselves of their services. The object of this disgusting operation, a kind of female factory-farming, was the insemination and subsequent pregnancy of the unfortunate girls with 'Aryan' blood. Thus Himmler hoped to breed a future society of Nazi supermen to be the true master race. Tall, blonde Nordic girls were forcibly enrolled and compelled to satisfy SS men, and to bear their children. At least it was restricted during the time of Nazi rule to women over the age of thirty, and single women at that. But had the Nazis triumphed, Himmler intended to extend it throughout the whole of the Reich.

> Every unmarried woman of thirty or over [Himmler said], will be required to report to the Lebensborn and put herself at their disposal, to be made pregnant. If she resists this order she will be punished as an enemy of the people. The SS will constitute themselves godparents to the children and the organisation will provide funds for their education.

Fortunately, the restriction to unmarried women of thirty and over enabled most German women to avoid entry into the Lebensborn. Marriage statistics shot up under Nazi rule, which, when the alternative was the Lebensborn, is hardly surprising. It was also an extremely inefficient organization, infant mortality among its nursing homes being twice the national average.[17]

Other obsessions of Himmler and his Occult Bureau included his belief that orthodox medicine was false. Herbalism was the only true medicine, he claimed. For this reason all the concentration camps had to have herb gardens attached to them. The inmates of the camps were instructed to collect enormous quantities of them for medicinal purposes.[18]

As well as herbalism, the SS and the Occult Bureau also engaged in such lunatic activities as trying to discover a Nordic strain of honey by importing 'Aryan' bees from the Himalayas; distilling a mineral water which cured all human illnesses; investigating the occult significance of the Etonian top hat and Gothic towers; the symbolism of the suppression of the Irish harp in Ulster; and the strength of the Rosicrucian fraternity.[19]

After a German bombing raid during the war on Oxford had failed to damage it, they even began an urgent inquiry into the magical properties of the bells of Oxford Cathedral, which had clearly been responsible for stopping the Luftwaffe from getting through.[20]

The German navy appears to have been officered largely by men who were both strongly pro-Nazi and also involved in any and every occult idea going. Not only did the navy enthusiastically support the hollow-earth doctrine until its eventual disproof as a result of the experiments of Fischer and his team with radar equipment; it also subscribed to other equally weird ideas. Radiaesthesia, better known as pendulum-swinging, was a particular source of interest to the German naval command.[21]

The navy's interest in radiaesthesia seems to have been sparked off by a letter from an occultist called Straniak. He claimed that from a photograph of a ship he could pinpoint its exact position within minutes. He held the photograph in one hand, the pendulum in the other on a silk thread. The pendulum was swung backwards and forwards across a chart of the oceans until its motion suddenly changed – or so at least Straniak claimed, and wrote to the navy to tell them so. Instead of filing his letter in the waste-paper bin, they invited Straniak to demonstrate his powers.[22]

Curiously enough, Straniak's pendulum was almost invariably accurate at detecting the location of the ship in the photograph. Excitedly, they speculated on whether this accounted for the British navy's success in hunting down German U-boats. At once Straniak was hired by the Naval Research Institute in Berlin to detect shipping. Before long he had a whole team of fellow occultists working under him, swinging their pendulums daily across maps of the Atlantic. As any psychic knows, however, such repeated attempts begin to induce a boredom factor, and after this intervened the results deteriorated dramatically. But the navy kept its faith with the pendulum-swingers, giving them choice food and wines, expensive cigars and every luxury they desired.

Along with the radiaesthetists, practitioners of Faustian pentagram magic and even mediums found themselves on the payroll of the German navy. But it was all to no avail, as their results got steadily worse and worse. Their failure to match expectations did not however, lead to the ending of the experiments. On the contrary, they continued right up to the time of the German surrender to the Allied forces.[23]

'I will tell you a secret,' Hitler told Rauschning, 'I am founding an order. It is from there that the second stage will emerge – the stage of the Man-God, when Man will be the measure and centre of the world. The Man-God, that splendid being, will be an object of worship. But there are other stages about which I am not permitted to speak.'[24]

Members of the SS were deliberately isolated from the rest of humanity. Their initiation took place in a series of stages, culminating in the notorious Ceremony of the Stifling Air. From this moment onwards, the SS member was dedicated body and soul to the commands of his order. As Hitler said,

> We do not want to do away with inequalities between men, but, on the contrary, to increase them and make them into a principle protected by impenetrable barriers. What will the social order of the future be like? Comrades, I will tell you: there will be a class of overlords, and after them the rank and file of Party Members in hierarchical order, and then the great mass of anonymous followers, servants and workers in perpetuity, and beneath them, again all the conquered foreign races, the modern slaves. And over and above all these there will reign a new and exalted nobility of whom I cannot speak. But of all these plans the ordinary militant members will know nothing.'[25]

Hitler, in short, planned to rule the earth as Vice-Regent of the Powers of Darkness. The concentration camps were based as much on his Satanism as his racism, for the inmates were held to belong to the class of slaves, and as such their only function was to serve the master race, itself serving the ends of the Dark Gods of the Cosmos.[26]

Among other lunatic activities which the Occult Bureau contemplated were stealing the Holy Grail![27] And it was Hielscher who had first suggested to Himmler the setting-up of such an organization. When the SS Colonel Sievers, who had been responsible for collecting the skulls of Jewish-Bolshevik commissars, was sentenced to hang at Nuremberg, it was Hielscher who gave him the last rites. On the gallows, Sievers and Hielscher said the prayers peculiar to their own Satanic religion, one which Hielscher himself had been largely instrumental in drafting. This man, who was directly and indirectly responsible for untold suffering to countless millions, was not disturbed by the Nuremberg judges. He gave evidence on Sievers's behalf at his trial, but was not touched himself.[28]

Another instance of occult activities that actively hindered the course of the war for Germany relates to the V-1 and V-2 rockets. Hitler placed great faith in them and to some extent was justified in doing so. The V-2 was the direct ancestor of the present intercontinental ballistic missiles, and its early use might well have resulted in the Allies undergoing such devastation that a separate peace might have been possible.

With Germany in a desperate military situation, and the miracle weapons ready to hand, one might have thought that the utmost urgency in their development and use was called for. The British certainly feared them enough to take strong action as soon as they learned of their existence. The factory at Peenemünde which made them was repeatedly bombed by the RAF, holding back production by several months. But, though they could hardly have guessed it at the time, the British had an unexpected ally in Hitler himself.

Hitler, who was nothing if not superstitious, dreamed one night not only that the V-2 would not work but that his Satanic overlords would exact retribution from him if he brought the rockets into action. Overruling the furious protests of the engineers, he ordered an immediate suspension of work on the new weapons. This lasted for two whole months. Even when Hitler had been persuaded finally that the rockets should at least be tested, he insisted that further experiments be carried out in the light of Hoerbiger's world ice theory. Hitler, like many other Hoerbigerians, was worried that the rocket tests might interfere with the balance in the universe between fire and ice and unleash a global disaster. As a result of all these various occult hold-ups, together with determined bombing raids by the RAF and deliberate acts of sabotage by the slave-labourers who worked on the rockets, the V-1 and V-2 eventually came into operation much too late to have any chance of influencing the ultimate course of the war. Here again, as with the occult-racial

Nazi theories, the very ideas which sustained the magical cosmogony of the Nazi state helped fatally to undermine its foundations.

19 The Twilight of the Gods

We have already recounted the influence that a German astrologer named Wulf had over Himmler. But, in the last two years of the war, his advisory role combined with that of Felix Kersten, another occultist, played a significant part in drawing Himmler away from under Hitler's Satanic spell.

Kersten was born in Finland, but had spent most of his life in Holland. He had studied the art of massage in his homeland as a young man, together with a technique that involved the manipulation of the nerve centres. This technique is based on the theory that physical pain can be the result of stress, and that by manipulation of the nerve centres, relaxation and relief from pain can result.[1]

Kersten moved to Berlin, where he became a successful masseur. There, he made the acquaintance of an oriental occultist and masseur called Ko, who taught Kersten many techniques he had not even suspected existed. Ko also told Kersten that his own horoscope had predicted, thirty years before, that he would meet a man in the West who would become his pupil in the healing arts.[2]

Though Ko was Chinese, he had received his training in Tibet. As we know, the Nazis had gone to great lengths to become involved with the Tibetan black lodges. But Ko was involved with the systems of white magic within Tibet. Over a period of months he taught Kersten techniques, not only of manipulation, but of meditation. As a result, when he laid his hands upon a patient it was as if a flow of energy came out of his fingertips and into the supine body. He found that, simply by laying on hands, he could diagnose illness in a patient, and then treat it by passing some of his own vital forces into the sufferer's body.[3]

Kersten prospered to such an extent that he became personal physician to the Dutch royal family. But one day in 1938 he received an invitation to meet the head of the SS and Gestapo, Himmler. Kersten was rigid with fear; he agonized over what to do, considering escape or even simply refusing. But, in the end, he went.[4]

Himmler had always suffered from stomach cramps, which by 1938 had become excruciating. Having heard of Kersten's powers, he wanted the Finnish masseur and occultist to heal him. Kersten told Himmler to lie down and then laid his hands upon him. He quickly discovered that Himmler was suffering from an acute disturbance of the nervous system – luckily it was a condition he could treat and within a few minutes, the pain was gone. Himmler was intensely grateful and begged Kersten to become his personal doctor. After some consideration, Kersten agreed. From now on Himmler would not go anywhere without taking his masseur with him.[5]

In 1941 Hitler told Himmler to implement plans for the Final Solution. Deeply disturbed, he told Kersten: 'I never wanted to destroy the Jews. I had quite different ideas. But Goebbels has it all on his conscience. Up to the spring of 1940, Jews could still leave Germany without any trouble. Then Goebbels got the upper hand.' Himmler apparently had wanted to send the Jews into exile, leaving them in full possession of their property. But Goebbels, he said, believed that the only answer was complete extermination.[6]

Surprised to hear such sentiments expressed by Himmler, Kersten set to work. He had to be cautious at first, but by July 1942 he was already beginning to have some success in getting Himmler to delay the genocide programme. In that year Himmler flew to Finland with Kersten where the latter met with the Finnish foreign minister. Kersten set out to sabotage the programme for the extermination of Finnish Jews. Following Kersten's advice, the Finnish foreign minister told Himmler that the Jewish problem was much too important to be decided without consulting parliament. But parliament did not meet for another five months, so the question would have to wait. Six months later Himmler brought up the matter again, but this time Kersten told him that the war situation was so grave that the recall of the Finnish parliament would be dangerous – especially with such a controversial item on the agenda. But perhaps the time would be right later on, much later. Though by now Himmler realized that Kersten was trying to sabotage the whole project, he only grumbled and did nothing. The masseur and occultist had saved the lives of the Jews in Finland at least.[7]

By 1944 Kersten felt sufficiently confident openly to challenge Himmler to end the genocide. According to an eyewitness, at a dinner in 1944 he 'worried away like a terrier until Himmler finally agreed to make a fundamental change in the whole Jewish business – in favour of the Jews'.[8]

As early as 1942 Kersten had openly urged Himmler to depose Hitler and conclude a separate peace with the Allies. But Himmler was still too much a man in the shadow of Hitler to contemplate such a radical step. In the winter of 1942, however, Kersten found an invaluable ally in his attempts to influence Himmler away from Hitler's Satanic influence. Enter once more the astrologer Wulf ...[9]

Wulf did not like Kersten, but he trusted him. With a great air of secrecy he showed the masseur his horoscope for Hitler. Saturn, Wulf explained, produced a malevolent effect upon Hitler, just as it had upon Napoleon: the latter's invasion of Russia was astrologically doomed, just like Hitler's. Kersten was impressed by both Wulf's astrological expertise and his political courage. He promised Wulf protection from the attentions of the Gestapo. Kersten also asked Wulf to produce a horoscope for himself. After this meeting Wulf became the official astrologer for the SS. The masseur gave him the information he needed to prepare his charts, and the astrologer returned the completed horoscope. Kersten, in his turn, gave the results of Wulf's calculations to Himmler for his perusal and decision.[10]

Over the next two years Kersten and Wulf worked tirelessly to persuade Himmler to overthrow Hitler and make a separate peace with the Western powers. This would certainly have been possible by that date, with most of the German army still out of the country, the Gestapo and SS under Himmler's personal command and with a strong anti-Nazi feeling growing among the German generals, most notably Rommel. But, try as they might, Himmler refused to betray his leader, even though he agreed with Kersten and Wulf's analysis.

Then, on 22 July 1944, a crisis developed in Himmler's affairs.[11] Two days previously the unsuccessful plot to blow up Hitler – masterminded by Generals Beck and Rommel – had failed. Himmler asked Kersten to order Wulf to produce a horoscope on the political consequences of the bomb plot for his own career. The SS Reichsführer had apparently been strongly criticized by Hitler for not foreseeing the plot, and was now out of favour.[12]

Kersten seized the opportunity this gave him to press on with his suggestions that Himmler should overthrow Hitler and try to make peace with the West. Within three months he had managed to persuade Himmler that his best chance of getting the Western powers to agree to a separate peace was to put a stop to the massacre of Jews. Himmler, at Kersten's insistence, had a meeting with the president of the Swiss Altbund in October 1944, the purpose of which was to discuss plans to put a stop to the persecution and killing of Jews by the Nazis.[13]

There, Himmler agreed to release all the Jews at present in German hands and to let them travel to Switzerland and safety. The meeting took place in Vienna; and on his return, Himmler gave immediate orders that no further acts of genocide against the Jews were to be carried out. He also instructed that all prisoners in concentration camps should be given food and medical attention. Two months later he agreed to another suggestion of Kersten's: that all Scandinavian prisoners then held in concentration camps be moved to a camp at Hamburg, fed by the Swedish Red Cross and then released into Sweden and freedom. The transport arrangements were made by the vice-president of the Swedish Red Cross.[14]

Once he had taken such unprecedented action, Himmler got nervous again. Kersten and Wulf pacified him, and this time summoned the SS Colonel Schellenberg to their assistance. The three of them again urged Himmler to overthrow Hitler and open negotiations with the West. In January 1945 they tried to set up a meeting between Himmler and Count Bernadotte of Sweden.[15]

Wulf was instructed by Kersten and Schellenberg to draw up a horoscope for both Himmler and Germany which would persuade the SS leader to take this course of action. Kersten left Wulf and Schellenberg to work away on Himmler, while he went off to Sweden for five weeks. When he came back he had a list of Jewish and Scandinavian prisoners given to him by an official of the World Jewish Congress. He urged Himmler to release them at once.[16]

Eight days of frantic negotiations began. Himmler was willing to release some but not all of the prisoners. He was terrified that if he released all of them Hitler would find out and exact a terrible revenge. Using his second string, Kersten approached Wulf once more and tried to persuade him to draw up yet another horoscope, which would show that if Himmler released the Jews, the World Jewish Congress would make representations on his behalf to the British and Americans. Wulf, however, refused. He would not draw up any horoscope except one 'indicated by astrological practice'. Besides, he added, the release of a few thousand Jews was only a minor matter; the important thing was to end the insane war.[17]

In spite of Wulf's unexpected stickiness, Kersten still arranged a meeting between himself, Himmler and Wulf. Wulf said that there were no astrological objections to the release of the Jewish prisoners. However, the portrait he painted of Germany's future was a desperate one. Himmler mumbled a few soothing noises about the effect of the V-2 on the course of the war and the meeting broke up indecisively. Next month, however, Himmler asked Schellenberg to convene another meeting. This time he handed Wulf a list of names and birth-dates with a view to their possible suitability for inclusion in a new German government. Three days later, while Wulf was still busy with his calculations, Kersten brought another Zionist representative to meet Himmler.[18]

The Zionist representative was introduced by Himmler to his masseur and his astrologer. Next day this unlikely group was joined by Schellenberg, and a list of prisoners to be released was discussed among the five of them. Schellenberg felt that Himmler should not agree to the release of prisoners without being given a guarantee of his own position. The Swedes, he suggested, should arrange a meeting between Himmler and the American General Eisenhower. He also wanted the Swedish government to guarantee free passage for German troops to return to Germany from Norway. After a day of discussions, Himmler agreed to all the Zionist demands and asked only that Eisenhower should be sounded out on the prospects of a meeting between the two of them. In the mean time he issued immediate orders to stop the killing of concentration camp prisoners.[19]

The Western powers told Count Bernadotte to inform Himmler that his proposals for a separate peace were completely unacceptable. Furthermore, his plan for a rendezvous with Eisenhower fell by the wayside. Wulf, by this time deeply depressed, was called upon for further astrological calculations, and within an hour he told Schellenberg that he would travel to Sweden for fresh negotiations with Bernadotte. Himmler's best course of action, Wulf told him, was to hide out and disguise himself as a farm labourer. After much discussion Himmler agreed to let Schellenberg go to Sweden. However, his own plans were uncertain. In consultation with Wulf, he considered which part of Germany was most suitable as a place for him to hide. Before long, Wulf made his own escape.[20] Himmler disguised himself as a member of the military field police. Captured by British patrols, he admitted his true identity and killed himself by taking poison. So ended the life of a man who had done more than most to bring misery and death upon millions of people during his brief career.[21]

As for Kersten, he was investigated on charges of possible complicity in war crimes and resoundingly vindicated. His services to humanity, the commission of inquiry decided, were without precedent. Incredible as it may seem, it was largely due to Kersten and, to an extent, Wulf that the extermination programme was temporarily halted. The change of heart on Himmler's part was entirely owing to the fact that Hitler's Satanic influence on him was being countered by the white magic of Kersten.[22]

By April 1945 every German knew that the war was finished. But, in the Berlin bunker, Hitler and his inner circle brooded darkly over a possible magical way out of their situation. Hitler knew that he had no military hope for victory now, and in his desperation he turned to the ultimate remedy of a black magician caught up in extremity – he formed a pact with Satan.

We, of course, do not have to believe in Satan ourselves to agree that many people do. Hitler, clearly, was one of those who did believe. Under the terms of a Satanic pact, the magician agrees to pay the Devil a price in return for his infernal help.[23] The usual price is either the magician's own soul or a blood sacrifice. And, since Hitler had sworn his soul to Satan years ago, only blood sacrifice remained open to him.

In this mood of despair and anger, Hitler screamed at his remaining generals: 'Losses can never be too high! They sow the seeds of future greatness.' Hitler summoned Speer in order to give him orders for a policy of complete destruction. 'If the war is to be lost,' he told Speer, 'the nation will also perish. There is no need to consider the basis of even a most primitive existence any longer. On the contrary, it is better to destroy even that and to destroy it ourselves.'[24]

Hitler gave orders that every town and factory in Germany was to be burned to the ground. All bridges were to be blown up, all dams undammed, all rolling-stock and coaches destroyed – indeed everything was to be smashed by the iron fist. Speer, despite being ordered to implement this insane policy, balked at the idea. Not being a magician, only a civil servant, he did not understand that Hitler had made a pact with Satan and that the sacrifice of the German people was the price he was offering in return. Speer simply agreed and then promptly failed to carry out Hitler's orders. Even so, Hitler did manage to murder large numbers of people. We have seen already how he ordered the flooding of the Berlin underground, as a result of which, 300,000 people lost their lives. He gave instructions that all remaining prisoners be killed, and that his own brother-in-law and his former surgeon be murdered. All traitors were to be immediately executed. As Trevor-Roper puts it: 'In his last days, Hitler seems like some cannibal god, rejoicing in the ruin of his own temples. Like an ancient hero, Hitler wished to be sent with human sacrifices to his grave.'[25]

In spite of Hitler's attempt to buy Satanic assistance by his final frenzied orgy of death and destruction, the military position worsened. Many Nazi leaders left Berlin on the night of 20 April. But Hitler stayed behind, still frantically working on magical escape routes from his situation. Next day, he made his last attempt. SS General Steiner was ordered to launch one last attack against the Russians now pouring into the streets of Berlin. Hitler used the troops as visualization aids, magically manipulating their movements in the vain hope of throwing back the Russian troops. For a whole day there was fierce fighting between the German and Russian forces; and then the inevitable happened. The following day saw the Germans repulsed and the Russians break through their lines.[26]

Hanna Reitsch, the famous German woman pilot, then flew into Berlin. Hitler told her then that he intended to commit suicide. The date was 22 April; there was no longer any point in delaying his decision. Yet still Hitler hung on.

By 26 April Russian shells were within range of the bunker itself. Yet still Hitler did nothing. He had told Reitsch that he did not want his body to fall into the hands of the Russians and be used as the Italians had used Mussolini's body. But still he waited.

Two days later he married Eva Braun, thus possibly fulfilling a prophecy of Nostradamus. He also wrote his political testament. Hitler was waiting for something – but what?[27]

Two days later the answer at last became plain. After lunch on 30 April, Hitler and Eva Braun shook hands with the rest of the inhabitants of the Berlin bunker. Then the two of them retired. She took poison, while Hitler shot himself.

Even in death Hitler had remained true to his dark religion.

He had seen to it that his suicide should coincide with and be a sacrifice to the powers of darkness. For 30 April is the old festival of Walpurgis Night, the most important date in the Satanic calendar. Even in death, Hitler had vowed eternal faithfulness to the Prince of Darkness.

The old Norse kings had liked to die at sea, gouging runic wounds into their bodies and then setting their ships on fire. On the death of Hitler, the SS burnt his body with petrol among the ruins of his blazing capital. Like an old Viking sacrifice to the gods, like the Satanic sorcerer burning at the stake, Hitler's very end was to be an occult, magical one.

Two days later the fighting was over. Hitler, National Socialism, and the Satanic ideology which had been the powerhouse driving a whole nation to destruction were finished at last. Even in death he had served Satan; but the powers he had raised against him were greater than he or even his enemies knew. By his magical acts he had drawn down upon himself the opposition of every white magician, every occultist not wholly depraved, in the rest of the world. No one, not even as skilled a black magician as Hitler, could confront so much power. For a time darkness may blot out the face of the sun, and an eclipse follow; but light is stronger than darkness, and will always triumph over it.

20 ⌐ Occult Opposition to the Nazis

As we have described in considerable detail throughout the book, the Nazis were involved in occult activities over a period of many years, covering an astonishing range of occult pursuits. But it was not only the Nazis who engaged in occult warfare.

We have already seen how British Intelligence recruited Louis de Wohl as the official astrologer to the government.[1] We have also seen how Stein became Churchill's official occult adviser.[2] But the British in particular made almost as much use of occultists as the Germans. From the beginning of the Second World War the British government was actively making use of all sorts of occult knowledge as possible war weapons. And, of course, there were magical and occult groups and individuals within Britain who took their own private steps to counter the menace from the occult Nazi state.

Between 1936 and 1939 the greatest (if also the most notorious) British magician and occultist of the twentieth century, Aleister Crowley, paid a number of visits to Germany. He had an exhibition of his paintings in Berlin and he certainly built up a number of German occult contacts over many years.[3] We know in particular that Martha Kunzel repeatedly urged on Hitler the wisdom of adopting Crowley's *The Book of the Law* as his guide. But in spite of Kunzel's pro-Nazi sentiments, she was unable to persuade him to do so. Hitler wanted *Mein Kampf* as the only holy book in Germany. And yet there are so many striking sentences in Rauschning's account where Hitler is – often word for word – paraphrasing or expressing an idea from *The Book of the Law*. We also know that Kunzel performed a Crowleyan ritual, after which she declared that Hitler was her 'magical child'. But Crowley, in spite of his visits to Nazi Germany, did not share her admiration for Hitler or the Nazis. He warned Kunzel that Britain would not stand for Hitler's behaviour indefinitely and that the brutality of the Third Reich was not at all in line with Crowley's own religion. The Nazis, for their part, had banned the German branch of his own magical order and most of its members were in concentration camps. In spite of Kunzel's continued admiration for Hitler, Crowley told her bluntly, when war broke out, that 'Britain would knock Hitler for six'.[4]

Now the curious thing is that, on the outbreak of the Second World War, the Director of Naval Intelligence invited Crowley to visit him. It is quite possible that Churchill, recently appointed as head of the navy, had a strong hand in arranging the interview. In any event, this meeting actually took place, and as a result of Crowley's advice two magical signs were adopted to boost British morale.[5] The first of these was used particularly by Churchill, who, as we have seen, was steeped in occultism; it was, of course, the famous V-sign. In magical terms, this is the antidote to the reversed swastika. Crowley's second magical contribution to the war effort was his introduction of the thumbs-up sign during the desperate days of 1940 when Britain stood alone, with only her coastline standing between her and the German army. This second sign is the sign of victory and of sexual magic.[6]

In the summer of 1940 the Germans had made themselves masters of Western Europe. Only Britain held out against them. With the retreat of the British army from Dunkirk, it was clearly only a matter of time before German troops started pouring across the Channel. Hitler certainly thought so, and so did the British. So did neutral observers, like the Americans.

By July the Germans had begun plans for 'Operation Sealion', the proposed invasion of Britain. There was no doubt that if they had landed the British army would have been defeated and the whole course of human history altered. Before long the Battle of Britain was raging and the British, though inflicting heavy casualties upon the Luftwaffe, were losing the war. It seemed only a matter of time before the RAF was destroyed and the German army invaded and conquered Britain. By September the British were in a desperate way and in Berlin Hitler was openly boasting: 'In England they're filled with curiosity and keep asking – "Why doesn't he come?" Be calm, be calm – he's coming! He's coming!'

But, of course, he never did come. Orthodox historians are unable to offer any credible reason for such an astonishing failure on Hitler's part to follow up his advantage. None of their suggestions holds any water at all. But there are other explanations available at which orthodox historians will not even look; they ought to be examined more closely. For there were many people within Britain, both individuals and members of occult and magical groups, who worked hard to defeat the Nazis by the use of occult powers.

In the first place, there were men like Stein, de Wohl and Crowley, all three of whom seem to have played key roles in the British war effort. Stein actually managed to obtain the plans of 'Operation Sealion', which must have helped Churchill considerably to prepare the nation's defences against a German landing. In the second place, there was the prime minister himself. To judge from his powers of oratory and his ability to inspire and influence people, Churchill was no mean master of the 'word-sword' himself. And the occult training he had received from the Druids[7] and the Illuminati[8] must have enabled him to work magic on his own account in defence of the country he loved.

The Druids, of course, represented a magical tradition stretching back long before the Romans. Even Pythagoras was taught his occult learning by Abaris, a Druid from Britain. In spite of all efforts by the Romans to destroy Druidism, they failed, although they did weaken its hold as an organized cult. It survived as a loose semi-underground movement, having the ability to adapt and disguise itself as something else. It survived both covertly, especially in the Celtic Church and through the Culdee monks, and openly, in the form of pagan rituals and philosophy taught to initiates.[9]

In 1171 Prince Hywel of Gwynedd was initiated into the Lesser Mysteries of Ceridwen, chief goddess of the Druids. And as late as 1538, the high priest of Hu Gadarn, their chief god, was burnt at the stake at Smithfield for worshipping the faith. And the Druid movement has survived as an underground cult right into the twentieth century.[10] The Druids were British, their island was under attack, and from a country whose leaders were arrant practitioners of black magic. With the prime minister a former member of the order, and Britain in its direst hour of need, what was more logical than that the Druids should seek to perform occult rites and ceremonies to keep the Nazis at bay? And this is exactly what they did.

In Wales and on the Isle of Man two ceremonies were held, one on Lammas Night, the other at Hallowe'en. At these ceremonies the Druids concentrated on throwing a protective shield around the islands of Britain and sending out rays of force to turn back the aggressors before they landed. Bombarding the German invasion barges with psychic energies, the Druids put into their enemies' minds the idea of retreat, of the impossibility of carrying out the invasion plan successfully. The Arch-Druid and his helpers put everything they had into this ritual, and it was successful.[11] Or, at least, Hitler did not pursue his invasion plans; and no good reason exists for his failure to do so. Here we have an explanation which makes sense, about rituals which actually happened, and which were designed to achieve a specific result. When that result was achieved, and orthodox historians are unable to give a satisfactory account of it, perhaps we should believe the testimony of those men and women who performed, under the shadow of darkness, the rites of power that saved the island when all seemed lost.

Another group of people, equally patriotic, equally passionate about the triumph of white magic over black, and who also took part in the occult defence of the island, were the witches. There is no doubt that Margaret Murray's theory of witchcraft as a continuous organized cult stretching from the Stone Age to the present day is too extreme a position to be adopted.[12] On the other hand, the idea put forward by Hugh Trevor-Roper that the Inquisition simply invented the witch-cult is also untenable.[13] There is no doubt that pagan rituals, as we have already seen with Druidism, occurred with great frequency. But it seems likely that the revival of witchcraft is largely the result of the activities of a charismatic nineteenth-century witch, George Pickingill. He founded a number of covens which survived him and became widely distributed around Britain. From the covens he founded, other offshoots were formed and thus the witch cult spread further afield.[14]

One of these 'splinter covens' was based in the New Forest, and whose leading light came to be an enigmatic character known as Gerald Brosseau Gardner who settled in Hampshire with his wife in 1936. With the imminent arrival of the Second World War, Gardner – who was fifty-five at the time – not only became active himself in Civil Defence, but also wrote to the *Daily Telegraph* to make a startling proposal which infuriated the Nazis.

Gardner pointed out that, under Magna Carta, every freeborn Englishman was entitled to bear arms for the defence of his family and his country. He suggested that an armed force of civilians be created to help defend Britain against the threat of Nazi invasion. A German newspaper called Gardner's suggestion 'an infringement of international law', but before long the British government formed the Local Defence Volunteers, better known as the Home Guard. Thus even the Home Guard was formed as a result of the promptings of an occultist.[15]

For Gardner was steeped in occult lore and learning. He was already known as the author of a book on the history and folklore of the Malay *kris*, a weapon used in Malaya. He belonged to a Rosicrucian fraternity in Hampshire, known as the Fellowship of Crotona. One of the members of this fellowship, Mabel Besant-Scott, was the daughter of Annie Besant, who had succeeded Blavatsky as the leader of Theosophy. This woman belonged not only to the Fellowship of Crotona but also to Co-Masonry, a form of Freemasonry which is not recognized by the English Grand Lodge. Becoming friendly with her, Gardner discovered that behind the front of Co-Masonry, she was actively involved in a functioning coven of witches, in the New Forest.[16]

Gardner found, on his admission to the coven, that most of its members were extremely elderly. He became alarmed at the prospect of the religion which immediately attracted him being in severe danger of dying out. Some years later this fear was to lead him into betraying his oath of secrecy and publishing two books on the history, rituals and beliefs of witchcraft. But that lay in the future. It was then 1940, and Gardner was a junior member of a coven of witches, all of whose members were deeply concerned about the anticipated invasion of Britain.

It was Lammas Night, 1940. France had fallen, and German troops were assembling across the Channel in preparation for an invasion of Britain. At this dark time in English history, the coven met in the New Forest to perform a magical ceremony, at which Gardner was an eyewitness and participant. Let us describe what happened next in his own words.

> Witches did cast spells, to stop Hitler landing after France fell. They met, raised the great cone of power and directed the thought at Hitler's brain: 'You cannot cross the sea,' 'You cannot cross the sea,' 'Not able to come,' 'Not able to come.' Just as their great-grandfathers had done to Boney and their remoter forefathers had done to the Spanish Armada with the words: 'Go on,' 'Go on,' 'Not able to land,' 'Not able to land.' I am not saying that they stopped Hitler. All I say is that I saw a very interesting ceremony performed with the intention of putting a certain idea into his mind, and this was repeated several times afterwards; and though all the invasion barges were ready, the fact was that Hitler never even tried to come.[17]

The occult historian Francis King has researched Gardner's story and discovered that there really was a witches' coven in the New Forest at the time and that it really did perform a magical ceremony designed to stop Hitler.[18] And, in spite of his disclaimer, Gardner is also claiming that the witches *did* stop Hitler.

King not only confirms that the New Forest coven existed and worked magic against Hitler; he also describes how, in order to aid the potency of the spell, a voluntary human sacrifice was undergone. Witches traditionally work their rites naked, but because of the climate in Britain, grease their bodies to keep out the cold. This time, however, the oldest and frailest member of the coven voluntarily left off his protective grease so that he might die during the ceremony and his life-force aid the power of the spell. Not only did he die during the ritual, but two other coven members died of pneumonia soon after.[19]

After the Lammas ceremony, the witches met three more times with the same intention, to stop Hitler. During the course of these ceremonies much psychic energy was expended by the elderly members of the coven. Six more members died as a result of their exertions, including the high priestess herself. But the magic had been successful; the Germans had indeed been stopped.[20]

One thing that modern parapsychologists have demonstrated beyond a shadow of a doubt is that the human mind is capable of influencing another mind even at distance. By the use of such techniques as telepathy and thought-transference, ideas and images can be planted within another person's mind.[21] Is it improbable, then, that their rituals, together with those performed by Druids and other occultists in the defence of this country, really did influence the mind of Hitler, and make him turn back when there was no reason in the world for him to do so? No rational explanation for the German retreat exists; but an occult one does, attested to by a number of eyewitnesses. Perhaps we would do well to ponder on the words of Hamlet: 'There are more things in heaven and earth, Horatio, than are dreamt of in your philosophy.'

Further occult protection was vested in this country by its possession of the Stone of Destiny, housed in Westminster Abbey, which many initiates believe to be the Grail Stone to which *Parsifal* alludes.[22]

Hitler also managed to provoke the occult opposition of the Romanies and, as we have already seen, the Kabbalistic Jews. What is hardly known at all, however, is that Stalin himself also employed a psychic to assist him.

The man in question was a Polish Jew called Wolf Messing. In 1937, before an audience of thousands, Messing made a prediction in a Warsaw theatre that Hitler would die if he turned towards the East. The furious Nazi leader reacted by putting a price of 200,000 marks on Messing's head.[23]

After the Nazi invasion of Poland, Messing was captured. However, he managed to hypnotize the police into assembling in one room, after which he locked the door and managed to escape into Russia, hidden inside a wagon carrying hay. Messing found himself in Stalin's Russia, a Polish Jew in exile, in a country which was at the time allied to Hitler. He did not even speak a word of Russian.[24]

In spite of these serious drawbacks, Messing applied to the Ministry of Culture for a job. 'We don't want fortune-tellers or sorcerers in this country,' they retorted. 'And telepathy doesn't exist!' Undeterred, Messing offered to provide them with a demonstration of his powers on the spot. This must have been impressive, for the Ministry of Culture promptly changed their minds and offered him a job. For a whole year he toured Russia, giving demonstrations of his psychic abilities in theatres.[25]

Within a year, right in the middle of a performance, Messing was interrupted by two men in the green uniform of the Soviet police. 'Come with us,' they told him. 'There is someone who wishes to meet you.' The men took Messing into a hotel, after which he was led into a room and told to wait. In a few minutes he came face to face with Stalin himself.[26]

With the grim humour for which he was noted, Stalin ordered Messing to carry out a psychic bank robbery. He was to walk into a Moscow bank, hand the cashier a blank piece of paper and mentally will the man to hand over 100,000 roubles. To everyone's amazement he actually managed to do it. When the cashier realized what he had done he fell to the floor in fear and had a heart attack. As Messing remarked, 'Luckily it wasn't fatal.'[27]

Messing's next assignment was to get out of the Kremlin without an exit pass, in full view of security guards. He was successful in this too, suggesting telepathically to the guards that he was an important official who did not need an exit pass.[28]

As if this was not enough, however, Stalin ordered him to perform one final psychic experiment. Messing had to get into Stalin's home without a pass, in full view of the secret police, the bodyguards and the armed security forces that were ever present. Several days later, Messing walked boldly into Stalin's office within his house. The Russian dictator stared at the Polish psychic in blank amazement.

'How did you manage that?' he asked him finally. 'It was easy,' Messing smiled. 'I kept mentally suggesting to the guards and servants, "I am Beria." So they let me in, of course.'

Beria was Stalin's chief of police and, after the dictator himself, the most feared man in the Soviet Union. But Messing did not look anything like Beria, nor had he attempted to disguise himself in any way. By using the power of mental suggestion alone, Messing had got Stalin's guards to let him in. After this, Stalin allowed the hypnotist every facility.[29]

In 1940, when Russo-German relations were perfectly

cloudless, the two countries having mounted a joint campaign against Poland which had resulted in its conquest and partition, Messing made an astonishing prediction. 'Soviet tanks,' he predicted, 'will roll into Berlin.' Hitler was furious, and the German Embassy launched an immediate protest. The Russians hesitated for a while over how to react, finally saying that they could not be responsible for the prophecies of Messing.[30]

Again in 1943, when the Germans were still on the offensive in Russia, and occupied the Crimea, the Baltic, the Ukraine and Byelorussia, Messing made another prediction. The war, he told a large audience in a theatre at Novosibirsk, would end in 1945, sometime during early May, which, of course, it did.[31]

The United States also took a great interest in occult matters, possibly because President Roosevelt was himself a Freemason. But it also owed quite a lot to the success of German occult activities.

Essentially it was hypnotism which they particularly wanted to investigate. In the late 1930s a Dr Wells from Syracuse University demonstrated that, under hypnosis, people could be forced to perform criminal actions. The US Army took an immediate interest in these results, and, during the war, American soldiers who showed reluctance were hypnotized into killing dummies under the impression they were Japanese soldiers.[32]

But the real pioneer of hypnotism as a weapon for use by the US government was Dr George Estabrooks, chairman of the Department of Psychology at Colgate University. Soon after Pearl Harbor, when the Japanese had sunk the American fleet, Estabrooks was summoned to the US War Department.

Estabrooks told them that men and women could be hypnotized into performing acts of sabotage, murder and intelligence-gathering without realizing that they were doing them. A hypnotic instruction to a single key officer could disrupt the operations of an entire army. Estabrooks showed how enemy generals could be hypnotized into making strategical blunders. And, as he pointed out, it would be possible for a trained hypnotist to create an entire army of saboteurs and Fifth Columnists within a country.

Estabrooks said that during World War I, a hypnotist offered to induce a captured U-boat captain into a trance, take his submarine through enemy mine-fields and make him attack the German fleet. The US Navy considered the idea but turned it down as too risky. In fact, said Estabrooks, it would have worked. Moreover, he added that scientists had now developed indirect methods of mind control which meant that it was unnecessary to hypnotize the ultimate target, only an intermediary. 'Personally,' Estabrooks continued, 'I am convinced that hypnosis is a bristling, dangerous armament which makes it doubly imperative to avoid the war of tomorrow.'[33]

During the years that followed the Estabrooks experiments, a number of US government agencies, principally those with intelligence functions, pursued secret research into hypnotic techniques. Their aims were twofold: to control and improve the mind. The Army too spent much time and money on hypnotizing a significant percentage of soldiers, in addition deliberately inducing amnesia in some. In this state they were made to carry out actions which they would not normally have done.[34]

Alarmed but also excited by the prospects which Estabrooks and his experiments had opened up to them, the US government placed 'scores of contracts' for research into hypnosis. Any research into behaviour control, belief-changing and conditioning was eagerly funded by the government. Out of this research was to come the Americans' own versions of brainwashing; 'mind control' was to become a particular obsession among the intelligence services.

The results of study into hypnosis by the Soviets were eagerly investigated, in particular an article by a certain Professor Luria. Luria described how he had been able to induce behaviour in a hypnotized subject which the person would not normally have carried out. Techniques of heightened relaxation and increased suggestibility were researched by the Americans, as well as the possibilities of hypnotic drugs.[35]

But the most amazing account of occult work undertaken by the Americans during the war is the so-called Philadelphia Experiment. According to Dr Morris Jessup, a man called Carlos Allende approached him in 1955 and told him, in two letters, of the tests. Allende said that in October 1943, the US

Navy had conducted an experiment on the Delaware River, which involved inducing a magnetic field on a destroyer in Philadelphia.

> The result was complete invisibility of a ship. Sailors on board the ship became semi-transparent to one another's eyes. The ship itself vanished from its Philadelphia dock and reappeared at its other regular dock at Newport, Virginia. Half the crew became insane. Some went into a semi-comatose state which Allende calls 'deep freezing'. They had to be exposed to another piece of electronic equipment to 'unfreeze' them. One man walked through the wall of his cabin in the sight of his wife and children, and vanished. Two more burst into flame as they were carrying compasses and burned for eighteen days. Other 'frozen' crew members were restored by laying on of hands.[36]

As it stands, the story sounds too far-fetched for words. But it is not quite so easy to dismiss as it first seems, for Jessup was summoned to the Office of Naval Research in Washington and shown a copy of his book with annotations in writing which he recognized as being Allende's. Three years later, Jessup was found dead – and only suicide or murder fit the facts.

Jessup had a belief that matter could be transported from one dimension to another through the use of magnetic fields. And, in the last year of his life, the Office of Naval Research approached Jessup to work on operations similar to the Philadelphia Experiment. He declined the invitation as being too dangerous, and not long afterwards was found dead. Was it because he knew too much about secret Navy projects? It is at least a possibility.

What is more, the Russians also give an account of the Philadelphia Experiment. According to the Russians, the Americans were experimenting with a magnetic field in the form of a Möbius Strip, a geometrical figure which has only one side, and no beginning or end. According to the Russian version, a submarine, not a destroyer, was involved in the experiments. Using an electronic device, the 'Möbius Strip was cut in two. The submarine promptly vanished from Philadelphia, reappearing instantaneously in Newport. Once again, a magnetic field was involved in the experiment.[37]

One thing which is immediately noticeable about the Russian

version is the absence of the hysterical and alarmist details which Allende supplies. All the Russians claim is that the experiment, designed to dematerialize and then rematerialize a naval vessel instantaneously at a different place, was successful. This is a sufficiently astonishing claim to render unnecessary all the bizarre and incredible detail with which Allende surrounded his own account.[38]

As can readily be seen, the amount of occult activity being undertaken during the war by both the Axis and the Allied powers was quite phenomenal. Millions were spent on projects which often achieved actual concrete results. Quite how the occult faculties work is still an open question; but that they do work is something that only the most hidebound 'rationalist' would deny. Only the ill-informed, dogmatic 'certainties' of positivism preclude a general recognition that there are certain awkward facts about the world which cannot be explained by our current theories.

Without doubt, there has been even more work done in the fields of parapsychology and occultism since the war than at any time in the history of the human race. Governments are not normally given to pouring billions into research which they regard as cranky or at best unlikely. In the last forty years, there has been a positive mushrooming of funding for such projects, both private and public. But it was the Second World War which first saw the widespread and systematic use of occult and magical techniques by governments as weapons of war.

Notes

1 Hitler's Youth

1 Louis Pauwels and Jacques Bergier, *The Morning of the Magicians* (Mayflower, 1973)
2 Ibid.
3 Ibid.
4 Bridget Hitler, *The Memoirs of Bridget Hitler* (Duckworth, 1970)
5 Francis King, *Satan and Swastika* (Mayflower, 1976)
6 Ibid.
7 James Webb, *The Occult Establishment* (Richard Drew, 1981)
8 Trevor Ravenscroft, *The Spear of Destiny* (Corgi, 1974)
9 Ibid.
10 Ibid.

2 The Spear of Destiny

1 From 'Absalom and Achitophel' (1681), a poem by John Dryden.
2 Ravenscroft, op. cit.
3 Ibid.
4 Ibid.
5 Walter Johannes Stein, *The Ninth Century and the Holy Grail* (Temple Lodge Press, 1988)
6 Ravenscroft, op. cit.
7 Read further on this matter in King, op. cit.; Bridget Hitler, op. cit.; Ravenscroft, op. cit.
8 Ravenscroft, op. cit.
9 Ibid.
10 Bridget Hitler, op. cit.

3 The Nazis and Astrology

1 Reinhard Heydrich, cited in King, op. cit.

2 Ibid.
3 Sheila Ostrander and Lynn Schroeder, *Psychic Discoveries behind the Iron Curtain* (Bantam, 1971)
4 King, op. cit.
5 The reason for the sustained campaign by the Nazis against the astrologers was partly a philosophical one – that astrology took account only of the individual and his or her birth sign, not their race or skin colour; and also because the Nazis, whose very birth had been conducted under occult auspices, feared and respected the Black Arts too much not to worry about its possible use against themselves. There was also, to an extent, a wish to appear more acceptable to middle-class Germans who regarded occultism as sheer nonsense. See King, op. cit.
6 J.H. Brennan, *Occult Reich* (Futura, 1974)
7 Ibid.
8 Louis de Wohl, *The Stars in Peace and War* (London, 1952)
9 This unknown astrologer was probably his son Albrecht Haushofer, a strong anti-Nazi. See King, op. cit.
10 King, op. cit.
11 Ibid.
12 Eric Russell, *A History of Astrology and Prediction* (New English Library, 1974)
13 King, op. cit.
14 Himmler was considering a *coup d'état* with the idea of replacing Hitler and concluding a separate peace with the West. See King, op. cit.
15 King, op. cit.

4 Racial Ramblings

1 For this subject, see further: Webb, op. cit.; and Richard Donington, *Wagner's 'Ring' and its Symbols* (Faber & Faber, 1969).
2 Webb, op. cit.
3 Wagner, cited in Ravenscroft, op. cit.
4 Webb, op. cit.
5 Ibid.
6 Ravenscroft, op. cit.
7 Ibid.
8 All quotations from Chamberlain come from his work, *The Foundations of the Nineteenth Century* (Munich, 1889)
9 Ravenscroft, op. cit.
10 Ibid.
11 Ibid.
12 King, op. cit.
13 Webb, op. cit.
14 Christine Stoddart (writing as 'Inquire Within'), *The Trail of the Serpent* (Boswell, 1936)
15 King, op. cit.
16 Webb, op. cit.

17 Ibid.
18 Brennan, op. cit.
19 Webb, op. cit.
20 Ibid.
21 Ibid.
22 Norman Cohn, *Warrant for Genocide* (London, 1970)
23 Ravenscroft, op. cit.
24 These quotations from Rosenberg are from his work *The Myth of the Twentieth Century* (Munich, 1934). It must be remembered that Rosenberg was the Nazi Party's official ideologist, so, far from being an unrepresentative crank, he represented the main stream of Nazi Party thinking.
25 Hermann Rauschning, *Hitler Speaks* (London, 1939)
26 Webb, op. cit.

5   The Thule Group

1 Webb, op. cit.
2 Ibid.
3 Ravenscroft, op. cit.
4 Ibid.
5 Ibid.
6 Brennan, op. cit.
7 Ibid.
8 Ravenscroft, op. cit.
9 Ibid.
10 King, op. cit.
11 Ravenscroft, op. cit.
12 Ibid.
13 Adolf Hitler, *Mein Kampf* (London, 1939)
14 Webb, op. cit.
15 King, op. cit.

6   One Foot in Atlantis

1 Rauschning, op. cit.
2 King, op. cit.
3 Ibid.
4 For more information on the *Oera Linda* book and Atland generally, see Robert Scrutton, *The Other Atlantis* (Sphere, 1977)
5 King, op. cit.
6 Ibid.
7 Ibid.
8 Ibid.
9 Ibid.

10 Ibid.
11 Webb, op. cit.
12 Ibid.
13 King, op. cit.
14 Scrutton, op. cit.
15 Lewis Spence, *Will Europe Follow Atlantis?* (Rider, 1940)
16 For further information on German researches into, and expeditions in search of, Atlantis, the following books are worth consulting: Nigel Pennick, *Hitler's Secret Sciences* (Neville Spearman, 1981); Charles Berlitz, *The Mystery of Atlantis* (Souvenir Press, 1969)

7 Fire and Frost

1 Brennan, op. cit.
2 King, op. cit.
3 H.S. Bellamy, *Moon, Myth and Man* (Faber & Faber, 1949)
4 H.S. Bellamy, *Built Before the Flood* (Faber & Faber, 1943)
5 Brennan, op. cit.
6 Webb, op. cit.
7 Brennan, op. cit.
8 Webb, op. cit.
9 Ibid.
10 King, op. cit.
11 Ibid.
12 Webb, op. cit.
13 King, op. cit.
14 Pauwels and Bergier, op. cit.
15 Ibid.
16 King, op. cit. The Talmud, of course, is one of the holy books of Judaism; the Edda is the sacred book of Norse paganism. The comparison was intended to show the superiority of Hoerbiger's theory over Einstein's by virtue of its 'Nordic' origins.
17 Webb, op. cit.
18 Ibid.
19 Brennan, op. cit.

8 Great Ball of Fire

1 John Grant and Colin Wilson (eds), *The Directory of Possibilities* (Webb & Bower, 1981)
2 Ibid.
3 Ibid.
4 Webb, op. cit.
5 King, op. cit.
6 Ibid.
7 Ibid.
8 Pauwels and Bergier, op. cit.
9 Webb, op. cit.

10 Pauwels and Bergier, op. cit.
11 King, op. cit.
12 Pauwels and Bergier, op. cit.

9   The Tibetan Connection

1 Ravenscroft, op. cit.
2 Stoddart, op. cit.
3 Geoffrey Ashe, *The Ancient Wisdom* (Abacus, 1978)
4 Ibid.
5 Webb, op. cit.
6 Ibid.
7 Ashe, op. cit.
8 Ibid.
9 Ravenscroft, op. cit.
10 Ibid.
11 Ibid.
12 Ibid.
13 Ibid.
14 Ibid.
15 Ibid.
16 Ashe, op. cit.
17 Ravenscroft, op. cit.
18 Ibid.
19 Ibid.
20 Ibid.
21 Ibid.
22 Webb, op. cit.
23 Pauwels and Bergier, op. cit.
24 Ibid.
25 Nicholas Roerich, *The Heart of Asia* (New York, 1930)
26 Stoddart, op. cit.
27 Roerich, *Altai-Himalaya* (Jarrolds, 1930)
28 Alec Maclellan, *The Lost World of Agharti* (Corgi, 1982)
29 Roerich, *The Heart of Asia*, op. cit.
30 Ferdinand Ossendowski, *Beasts, Men & Gods* (London, 1924)
31 Roerich, *Altai-Himalaya*, op. cit.
32 Ashe, op. cit.
33 Roerich, *Altai-Himalaya*, op. cit.
34 Brennan, op. cit.
35 Pauwels and Bergier, op. cit.
36 Maclellan, op. cit.

10   The Nazis and Flying Saucers

1 Ashe, op. cit. For those interested in pursuing the subject further, I recommend Rupert Furneaux, *The Tungus Event* (Panther, 1977)

2 Ashe, op. cit.
3 Ibid.
4 Roerich, *Altai-Himalaya*, op. cit.
5 Roerich, *Himalayas, Abode of Light* (David Marlowe, 1947)
6 Ibid.
7 Ashe, op. cit.
8 W.Y. Evans-Wentz, *The Tibetan Book of the Great Liberation* (Oxford University Press, 1954)
9 Alexandra David-Neel, *With Mystics and Magicians in Tibet* (Bodley Head, 1931)
10 Ashe, op. cit.
11 Andrew Tomas, *Shamballah: Oasis of Light* (Sphere, 1977)

11 Hitler as Conjuror

1 Brennan, op. cit.
2 King, op. cit.
3 Ibid.
4 Ibid.
5 Ibid.
6 Alan Bullock, *Hitler: A Study in Tyranny* (London, 1962)
7 Hugh Trevor-Roper, *The Last Days of Hitler* (London, 1947)
8 William Shirer, *The Rise and Fall of the Third Reich* (London, 1950)
9 Brennan, op. cit.
10 Ravenscroft, op. cit.
11 Ibid.
12 King, op. cit.
13 Richard Cavendish, *The Black Arts* (Pan, 1967)
14 Brennan, op. cit.
15 Ibid.
16 Ostrander and Schroeder, op. cit.
17 Maclellan, op. cit.
18 Edmund Shaftesbury, *Instantaneous Personal Magnetism* (Psychology Publishing Co., 1957)
19 Ravenscroft, op. cit.
20 King, op. cit.
21 Ibid.
22 Ibid.
23 Ibid.
24 Ibid.
25 Ibid.
26 Ravenscroft, op. cit.
27 King, op. cit.

12 Seeing into the Future

1 Immanuel Kant, *Critique of Pure Reason* (Wiley, 1943)
2 Brennan, op. cit.
3 Ibid.
4 Ibid.
5 Ibid.
6 Ibid.
7 Ibid.
8 Ibid.
9 Ibid.
10 Ibid.
11 Ibid.
12 Ibid.
13 Ibid.
14 Ibid.
15 King, op. cit.
16 Ibid.
17 Ravenscroft, op. cit.
18 Grant and Wilson, op. cit.

13 Nostradamus Speaks

1 Stewart Robb, *Prophecies on World Events by Nostradamus* (Liveright, 1961)
2 Ibid.
3 Ibid.
4 Ibid.
5 Ibid.
6 Ibid.
7 Ibid.
8 Ibid.
9 Ibid.
10 Ibid.
11 Ibid.
12 King, op. cit.
13 De Wohl, op. cit.
14 Robb, op. cit.
15 Ibid.
16 Ibid.
17 Ibid.

14 Numbers and the Nazis

1 Cavendish, op. cit.
2 Ibid.
3 Louis Hamon (writing as 'Cheiro'), *Cheiro's Book of Numbers* (Corgi, 1968)

4 Ibid.
5 Add A (1) D (4) O (7) L (3) F (8) H (5) I (1) T (4) L (3) E (5) and R (2) together. The result is 43. Add 4 and 3 together to produce 7.
6 Ibid.
7 King, op. cit.
8 In Cheiro's Chaldaean system, 20–4–1889 would be taken only as amplifying the birth-number. The important number is the 20, which would be seen as the birth-number. 20 is 2 + 0, which adds up to 2. In numerology, 2 and 7 always vibrate harmoniously together; if you prefer, they have an affinity for one another, like Cancer and Pisces, Taurus and Capricorn. If you add up 20–4–1889, you get 20 (the birth number being always computed separately) + 4 + 1 + 8 + 8 + 9 = 50 = 5.
9 Cavendish, op. cit.
10 Kurt Seligmann, *Magic, Supernaturalism and Religion* (Paladin, 1975)

15 A Clash of Symbols

1 Stoddart, op. cit.
2 King, op. cit.
3 Ravenscroft, op. cit.
4 Brennan, op. cit.
5 H.T.F. Rhodes, *The Satanic Mass* (Jarrolds, 1968)
6 Webb, op. cit.
7 Ibid.
8 Ibid.
9 Brennan, op. cit.
10 J.E. Cirlot, *A Dictionary of Symbols* (Routledge, 1983)
11 Ravenscroft, op. cit.
12 King, op. cit.
13 Ibid.
14 Pauwels and Bergier, op. cit.
15 Ravenscroft, op. cit.

16 Black Camelot

1 Willi Frischauer, *Himmler: The Evil Genius of the Third Reich* (Odhams, 1966); cited in Brennan, op. cit.
2 Ravenscroft, op. cit.
3 Ibid.
4 Ibid.
5 Ibid.
6 Ibid.
7 King, op. cit.
8 Ravenscroft, op. cit.
9 King, op. cit.

10 Ravenscroft, op. cit.
11 Brennan, op. cit.
12 Ravenscroft, op. cit.
13 Ibid.
14 Pauwels and Bergier, op. cit.
15 Brennan, op. cit.
16 Ibid.
17 Ibid.
18 Ravenscroft, op. cit.
19 Ibid.
20 Brennan, op. cit.
21 King, op. cit.
22 Ibid.

17   Bumps on the Head

1 Lyall Watson, *Supernature* (Coronet, 1974)
2 Ibid.
3 Ibid.
4 King, op. cit.
5 Ibid.
6 Brennan, op. cit.
7 Ibid.
8 King, op. cit.
9 Benjamin Walker, *Encyclopaedia of Esoteric Man* (Routledge, 1977)
10 King, op. cit.
11 Anne Petrie, *Your Psychic A–Z* (Arrow, 1984)

18   Among Murderers and Madmen

1 King, op. cit.
2 Ibid.
3 Ibid.
4 Ibid.
5 Ibid.
6 Ibid.
7 Ibid.
8 Ibid.
9 Ravenscroft, op. cit.
10 Ibid.
11 Ibid.
12 Ibid.
13 Ibid.
14 Ibid.
15 King, op. cit.

16 Pauwels and Bergier, op. cit.
17 King, op. cit.
18 Ibid.
19 Himmler seems to have believed that the British Secret Service was run by the Rosicrucians. See Michael Howard, *The Occult Conspiracy* (Rider, 1989)
20 Pauwels and Bergier, op. cit.
21 King, op. cit.
22 Ibid.
23 Ibid.
24 Rauschning, op. cit.
25 Pauwels and Bergier, op. cit.
26 Ibid.
27 King, op. cit.
28 Pauwels and Bergier, op. cit.
29 King, op. cit.

19   The Twilight of the Gods

1 Felix Kersten, *The Kersten Memoirs* (London, 1956)
2 Ibid.
3 Ibid.
4 Ibid.
5 Ibid.
6 Ibid.
7 Ibid.
8 Brennan, op. cit.
9 Ibid.
10 Ibid.
11 Ibid.
12 Ibid.
13 Kersten, op. cit.
14 Ibid.
15 Brennan, op. cit.
16 Ibid.
17 Ibid.
18 Ibid.
19 Ibid.
20 Ibid.
21 King, op. cit.
22 Kersten, op. cit.
23 Brennan, op. cit.
24 Ibid.
25 Trevor-Roper, op. cit.
26 Brennan, op. cit.
27 Ibid.

20   Occult Opposition to the Nazis

1 De Wohl, op. cit.
2 Ravenscroft, op. cit.
3 Gerald Suster, *The Legacy of the Beast* (W.H. Allen, 1988)
4 King, op. cit.
5 Suster, op. cit.
6 Ibid.
7 Winston Churchill was initiated into the Albion Lodge of the Ancient Order of Druids at Blenheim on 15 August 1908. See Stuart Piggott, *The Druids* (Thames & Hudson, 1968)
8 Dennis Wheatley, *The Devil and All His Works* (Peerage Books, 1983). Wheatley, of course, was a member of British Intelligence during the Second World War.
9 Isabel Hill Elder, *Celt, Druid and Culdee* (Covenant, 1973)
10 Piggott, op. cit.
11 Information on the Druid ceremonies comes from Druid sources communicated to the author in confidence. There is no doubt that these ceremonies took place, however. Although I know of no previous factual account of the Druid ceremonies, a fictional account of them is given in Dale Estey, *A Lost Tale* (Ace Books, 1982)
12 Margaret Murray, *The Witch-Cult in Western Europe* (Oxford University Press, 1921)
13 Hugh Trevor-Roper, 'The European Witch-Craze and Social Change' in Max Marwick (ed), *Witchcraft and Sorcery* (Penguin, 1970)
14 Janet and Stewart Farrar, *The Witches' Way: Principles, Rituals and Beliefs of Modern Witchcraft* (Robert Hale, 1984)
15 Brennan, op. cit.
16 Ibid.
17 Gerald Gardner, *Witchcraft Today* (Rider, 1954)
18 King, op. cit.
19 Ibid.
20 Ibid.
21 Walter Bowart, *Operation Mind Control* (Fontana, 1978)
22 John Matthews and Marian Green, *The Grail-Seekers' Companion* (Aquarian, 1986)
23 Ostrander and Schroeder, op. cit.
24 Ibid.
25 Ibid.
26 Ibid.
27 Ibid.
28 Ibid.
29 Ibid.
30 Ibid.
31 Ibid.
32 Bowart, op. cit.
33 Ibid.
34 Ibid.

35 Ibid.
36 Charles Berlitz and William Moore, *The Philadelphia Experiment* (Souvenir Press, 1979)
37 Robert Charroux, *The Mysterious Unknown* (Corgi, 1975)
38 Ibid.

Bibliography

Book details list either place of publication or name of publisher.

Ahmed, Rollo, *The Black Art* (Arrow, 1956)
Ashe, Geoffrey, *The Ancient Wisdom* (Abacus, 1979)
Bayley, Harold, *The Lost Language of Symbolism* (London, 1912)
Bellamy, H.S., *Built Before the Flood* (Faber & Faber, 1943)
———, *The Atlantis Myth* (Faber & Faber 1948)
———, *Moon, Myth and Man* (Faber & Faber 1949)
Bellamy, H.S. and Allen, Peter, *The Great Idol of Tiahuanaco* (Faber & Faber 1959)
Berlitz, Charles and Moore, William, *The Philadelphia Experiment* (Souvenir Press, 1979)
Bessy, Maurice, *A Pictorial History of Magic and the Supernatural* (Spring Books, 1972)
Blavatsky, H.P., *An Abridgement of 'The Secret Doctrine'* (Theosophical Publishing House, 1968)
———, *Studies in Occultism* (Sphere, 1974)
Bowart, Walter, *Operation Mind Control* (Fontana, 1978)
Brennan, J.H., *Occult Reich* (Futura, 1974)
Burland, C.A., *The Magical Arts* (Arthur Baker, 1956)
Carpenter, Edward, *Pagan and Christian Creeds* (Allen & Unwin, 1920)
Cavendish, Richard, *The Black Arts* (Pan, 1967)
Chetwynd, Tom, *A Dictionary of Symbols* (Paladin, 1982)
Cirlot, J.E., *A Dictionary of Symbols* (Routledge, 1983)
Cohn, Norman, *Warrant for Genocide* (London, 1970)
———, *The Pursuit of the Millenium* (London, 1968)
David-Neel, Alexandra, *With Mystics and Magicians in Tibet* (Bodley Head, 1931)
De Wohl, Louis, *The Stars in Peace and War* (London, 1952)
Donington, Richard, *Wagner's 'Ring' and its Symbols* (Faber & Faber, 1969)

Donnelly, Dorothy, *The Golden Well* (Sheed & Ward, 1950)

Eliade, Mircea, *The Myth of the Eternal Return* (Bollingen, 1974)

Gardner, Gerald, *Witchcraft Today* (Rider, 1954)

Gettings, Fred, *A Dictionary of Occult, Hermetic and Alchemical Sigils* (Routledge, 1981)

Gould, Rupert, *Oddities* (New York University Press, 1966)

Grant, John and Wilson, Colin (eds), *The Dictionary of Possibilities* (Webb & Bower, 1981)

Hitler, Adolf, *Mein Kampf* (London, 1939)

Hitler, Bridget, *The Memoirs of Bridget Hitler* (Duckworth, 1970)

Howe, Ellic, *Urania's Children* (William Kimber, 1970)

Kersten, Felix, *The Kersten Memoirs* (London, 1956)

Keyserling, Hermann, *Europe* (London, 1924)

———, *Travel Diary of a Philosopher* (London, 1925)

———, *Creative Understanding* (London, 1929)

———, *The Recovery of Truth* (London, 1929)

———, *The Art of Life* (London, 1937)

King, Francis, *Ritual Magic* (New English Library, 1973)

———, *Satan and Swastika* (Mayflower, 1976)

———, *Tantra for Westerners* (Aquarian, 1986)

La Vey, Anton, *The Satanic Bible* (Star, 1977)

Maclellan, Alec, *The Lost World of Agharti* (Corgi, 1982)

Magré, Maurice, *The Return of the Magi* (Sphere, 1975)

Matthews, John and Green, Marian, *The Grail-Seeker's Companion* (Aquarian, 1986)

Michelet, Jules, *Satanism and Witchcraft* (Tandem, 1968)

Ostrander, Sheila and Schroeder, Lynn, *Psychic Discoveries behind the Iron Curtain* (Bantam, 1971)

Pauwels, Louis and Bergier, Jacques, *The Morning of the Magicians* (Mayflower, 1973)

Petrie, Anne, *Your Psychic A-Z* (Arrow, 1984)

Poliakov, Leon, *The Aryan Myth* (New American Library, 1974)

Rauschning, Hermann, *Hitler Speaks* (London, 1939)

———, *The Revolution of Nihilism* (London, 1941)

Ravenscroft, Trevor, *The Spear of Destiny* (Corgi, 1974)

Rhodes, H.T.F., *The Satanic Mass* (Jarrolds, 1968)

Robb, Stewart, *Prophecies on World Events by Nostradamus* (Liveright, 1961)

Roberts, Anthony and Gilbertson, Geoff, *The Dark Gods* (Panther, 1980)

Roerich, Nicholas, *Altai-Himalaya* (Jarrolds, 1930)

———, *Himalayas, Abode of Light* (David Marlowe, 1947)

Russell, Eric, *A History of Astrology and Prediction* (New English Library, 1974)

Scrutton, Robert, *The Other Atlantis* (Sphere, 1977)

Seligmann, Kurt, *Magic, Supernaturalism and Religion* (Paladin, 1975)

Shaftesbury, Edmund, *Instantaneous Personal Magnetism* (Psychology Publishing Co., 1957)

Shirer, William, *The Rise and Fall of the Third Reich* (London, 1950)

Spence, Lewis, *Will Europe Follow Atlantis?* (Rider, 1940)

Stoddart, Christine (writing as 'Inquire Within'), *Light-Bearers of Darkness* (Boswell, 1931)

——, *The Trail of the Serpent* (Boswell, 1936)

Suster, Gerald, *The Legacy of the Beast* (W.H. Allen, 1988)

Symonds, John, *The Great Beast* (Macdonald, 1971)

Tomas, Andrew, *Atlantis: From Legend to Discovery* (Hale, 1972)

——, *Shamballah: Oasis of Light* (Sphere, 1977)

Trevor-Roper, Hugh, *The Last Days of Hitler* (London, 1947)

Valiente, Doreen, *An ABC of Witchcraft Past and Present* (Hale, 1973)

Walker, Benjamin, *Encyclopaedia of Esoteric Man* (Routledge, 1977)

Watson, Lyall, *Supernature* (Coronet, 1974)

Webb, James, *The Occult Establishment* (Richard Drew, 1981)

Wheatley, Dennis, *The Devil and All His Works* (Peerage, 1983)

Wilson, Colin, *Mysteries* (Granada, 1978)

——, *Access to Inner Worlds* (Rider, 1983)

——, *The Occult* (Panther, 1984)

Woolf, Leonard, *After the Deluge* (Pelican, 1937)

Index